Politics, Agricultural Development, and Conflict Resolution

An In-Depth Analysis of the Moyen Bani Programme in Mali

Chuku-Dinka R. Spencer

UNIVERSITY PRESS OF AMERICA,® INC.
Lanham • Boulder • New York • Toronto • Plymouth, UK

Copyright © 2012 by
University Press of America,® Inc.
4501 Forbes Boulevard
Suite 200
Lanham, Maryland 20706
UPA Acquisitions Department (301) 459-3366

Estover Road
Plymouth PL6 7PY
United Kingdom

All rights reserved
Printed in the United States of America
British Library Cataloging in Publication Information Available

Library of Congress Control Number: 2011936899
ISBN: 978-0-7618-5687-0 (paperback : alk. paper)
eISBN: 978-0-7618-5688-7

∞™ The paper used in this publication meets the minimum
requirements of American National Standard for Information
Sciences—Permanence of Paper for Printed Library Materials,
ANSI Z39.48-1992

The book is dedicated to my late parents,
Lemuel and Doris SPENCER,
and late parents-in-law,
John and Hortense BARBER

Contents

Illustrations   vii
Foreword   ix
Preface   xi
Acknowledgments   xiii
Abbreviations and Acronyms   xv

1 Introduction   1
2 Background   9
3 The Program   21
4 The Conflict   43
5 The Conflict and Post Conflict Period   79
6 Conclusion   93

Bibliography   101
Index   109

Illustrations

FIGURES

1.1.	Map of Mali Showing Major River Basins	4
2.1.	Fluctuations in Area Harvested in Cereals, 1990–2000	16
2.2.	Fluctuations in Cereal Production, 1990–2000	16
3.1.	Map of Program Area	29
3.2.	Map of Localization of Talo and Djenne Dams	30

TABLES

2.1.	Area Harvested in Thousand Hectares, 1990–2000	15
2.2.	Production of Cereals, in Thousand of Metric Tonnes, 1990–2000	17
3.1.	Summary of Estimated Cost of the First Phase by Component	33
3.2.	Summary of Financing Plan	34
5.1.	Implementation of Major Activities	80
5.2.	Summary of the Implementation Program of Key Activities	81
5.3a.	Annual Disbursement Schedule, AfDB	87
5.3b.	Annual Disbursement Schedule, OPEC Fund	87
5.3c.	Annual Disbursement Schedule, Government of Mali	88

Foreword

This is a complete, objective, and thorough study of the issues surrounding the controversial Moyen Bani Program in Mali. Chuku-Dinka draws on his professional experience and deep understanding of the development arena during the past thirty-five years. He explains clearly the roles of the parties involved and forms conclusions on the project itself and the international development process. His understanding of the program lifecycle enables him to re-examine the dam costs and benefits with careful analysis. His work is a welcome insight into the complicated issues surrounding the dam and the river basin. The analysis of the economic and social implications of the delays to the project, and the influence of the international sponsors and NGO are sensitively handled. Using concepts such as emotions, perceptions, high- and low-context cultures, he explains the positions taken by the parties in the conflict at different times during the resolution process. The conclusions offer lessons to a wide audience, especially those interested in how conflict impacts on development and development issues.

Michael J. Slater, Group Chairman,
MASDAR International

Preface

It is remarkable how powerful associated and suggested ideas can be in the mind of a reader. I embarked on the writing of this book while on retirement. I regularly read books and articles on development and development projects and the role non-governmental organizations (NGOs) play in development projects in developing countries. It was while I was reading one such article that I started to reflect on the various projects, in the many African countries, with which I was involved and in which extensive discussions were held with NGOs, both local and international. I drew up various circumstances in which NGOs interventions occurred.

I observed that NGOs often intervened in projects which they felt would negatively affect the social and/or physical environment. Their perceptions tended to be in opposition to those of the promoters, sponsors, or targeted population of the projects in the countries concerned. Take the case of a project in a southern African country during the height of the drought in that area in the 1990s. A group of international NGOs from various developed countries were campaigning for a major irrigation project not to be undertaken in the country concerned. They were doing so at the very time that rainfall had made itself very scarce in the region for several years. Why did the NGOs oppose the project? It was realized that their perceptions, past experiences, and their points of reference concerning the project were different from those of the target population. The concerns of the NGOs related mainly to the size of the project, especially the dam that was to be constructed and its social, health and environmental impacts. These were different from those of the population who had lost crops, livestock, and even lives to the drought, and for whom the future without the project, seemed at that time, very bleak. Such contrasting positions could lead to conflict. What factors influenced their perceptions? How did those factors affect the roles they have devolved upon themselves to play? What made them want to intervene in development projects? Did they appreciate the historical, geographic, administrative, political and economic backgrounds of the projects?

It would be instructive to delve into the whys and wherefores of the interventions of the NGOs in the developing countries. The perceptions, emotions, and past experiences which influenced the way they framed the issues with which they were concerned required a study. What effect did their interventions have on the expected and actual returns, outcomes, and impact of the projects? How did the government and the population in the developing countries view their interventions? Given the wide scope of the subject, it would be judicious to narrow the study down. I realized then that it would be worthwhile to explore this role through an in-depth analysis of a particular project. The idea of this book was nurtured. This particular program was unique as it was the subject of a protest which led to a protracted and seemingly intractable conflict. It had all the essential ingredients. These include local politics, local beliefs, public administration, local, and international NGOs, changes in perceptions, frames, *and* a conflict. I felt that this program would be an excellent example to analyze in-depth all these factors.

I am grateful to all my former colleagues in the agriculture departments of the African Development Bank, especially the project officers. During the period we worked together, they contributed to the strengthening of my conviction that rigorously designed, well-guided, thoroughly implementable, and flexibly managed projects with the farmers in the driver seat could contribute significantly and positively to the reduction of poverty in developing countries. "Implementable" includes the necessity of anticipating responses and reactions the project will elicit and catering for them in the design and/or at implementation.

Acknowledgments

My gratitude goes to the ALMIGHTY for making everything possible. My thanks go to my spouse, Waltina, sons, Chuku-Dinka, W, Chuku-Dima R, and Cheka R. Spencer for their constant support, encouragement, assistance and invaluable comments and suggestions. To my sister, Ethel Greene, and my nephew Raymond, I say thank you for your questions, and suggestions.

I would also like to thank my good friends, Sorie Conteh, Derris Jenkins-Johnston, and Esther Kasalu-Coffin, for their very useful comments and suggestions on the manuscript.

The views expressed are not necessarily those of any institution, past or present, with which the author may be or may have been associated. Any errors and omissions are the sole responsibility of the author.

Abbreviations and Acronyms

ADEMA	Alliance pour la Démocratie au Mali
AfDB	African Development Bank
AfDF	African Development Fund
AND	Association of Natives of Djenne
BC	Before Christ
BCE	Before Current Era
CE	Current Era
CFAF-CFA	Francophone African Community Franc
CGIAR	Consultative Group for International Agricultural Research
CILSS	Inter-Governmental Committee for the Fight against Drought in the Sahel
C.S	Cultural Survival
C.S.Q	Cultural Survival Quarterly
D.C	District of Columbia
D.F.I	Development Finance Institution
EIAS	Environmental Impact Assessment Study
ERR	Economic Rate of Return
Ex Ante	Intended or expected outcome before the event
Ex Post	Actual outcome after the event
FAO	Food and Agricultural Organization
FCFA	Francophone African Community Franc
GDP	Gross Domestic Product
GEF	Global Environment Facility
GNP	Gross National Product
HCCT	Haut Conseil des Collectivités Territoriales
IERR	Internal Economic Rate of Return
IMF	International Monetary Fund
INGO	International Non-Governmental Organization

IUCN	International Union for the Conservation of Nature
IWMI	International Water Management Institute
km²	Square Kilometer
m	meter
MCF	Millenium Challenge Fund
MDD	Mission de Décentralisation et de Déconcentration
MDRI	Mission de Décentralisation et des Réformes Institutionelles
mm	Millimeter
N/A	Not Applicable
NGO	Non-governmental Organization
OECD	Organization for Economic Co-operation and Development
OPEC	Organization of Petroleum Exporting Countries
PRSP	Poverty Reduction Strategy Paper
REDSO	Regional Economic Development Services Office
SSA	Sub-Saharan Africa
UNCTAD	United Nations Conference on Trade and Development
UNESCO	United Nations Educational, Scientific and Cultural Organization
US	United States
USA	United States of America
USAID	United States Agency for International Development
WARDA	West African Rice Development Association *now* African Rice Center
WB	World Bank

Chapter One

Introduction

Development programs are generally made up of two or more projects. They are the preferred vehicle, in both developed and developing countries, by which these countries channel activities which lead to development and growth. The Moyen Bani Program in Mali, made up of two phases, was one such program. In this book, the term "program" will be used consistently when referring to the Moyen Bani Program. Rural development programs and projects are intended to assist people to improve their living standards. Even though projects, in themselves, may be neutral, perceptions of their outcome and impact may vary from one person to another. This difference in perception, if not resolved, could lead to conflict. In the Moyen Bani Program, differences in perception between the upstream and downstream populations of the quantity of water flowing downstream, after the construction of a dam at Talo was the point of contention which led to a conflict.

In fact, differences in perceptions of where projects should be located are also sources of conflict. In many African countries, such as Nigeria and Sierra Leone of the 1960s, political considerations motivated the location of rural development projects irrespective of development needs.[1] This statement notwithstanding, it can be safely noted that the enormity of the economic and social development problems in many of these countries was and is such that almost all geographic locations needed development and more particularly rural development projects. This latter is relevant because agriculture is the dominant, and perhaps, the most sustainable and renewable sector in many of these countries. Which area receives priority in the decision making concerning the location often becomes a matter of politicking.

In the latter part of the 1990s such motivations, however, had not gone away and still significantly entered the decision equation concerning the location of development projects. It could be said though, that it would hardly be realistic, in the present political and development contexts of democracy, to ask politicians to cease from using their powers of resource allocation to enhance their popularity among their constituents and thus contribute towards acquiring votes. This is not peculiar to only developing countries. In the United States of America for example, the earmarks and "pork bellies", whereby funds are reserved for pet projects of congressional members, are expected to contribute to securing votes for these members. In the same vein, in 2009, in the United Kingdom, the Minister of Olympics in a campaign meeting for a general election candidate for Erith and Thamesmead, told the constituents that the area will benefit from substantial investment money under the vast amount available in the London 2012 Olympic Games Fund and that the candidate she was supporting, was the right person, as member of parliament, to maximize such benefits.[2]

No matter what factors entered the decision making concerning the location of development projects, it is important that politicians are aware of the responses projects will elicit. These responses are interrelated and form part of an integrated whole. They include responses related to the environment, the body politic, the economy and the society as well as the constituent sections and organizations of the society. The belief systems and local politics in the program area have also to be taken into consideration. Responses include how the program will affect these aspects and also how they will, in turn, affect the program. In addition, when projects and programs are being considered, the responses include the capacity of the institutions and bodies, in the public administration and private sector, to participate effectively in the implementation of the particular project or the overall program. Failure to fully comprehend and prepare for these responses could, in many cases, lead to serious setbacks in the implementation of the program. This, in turn, would jeopardize the outcome and impact expected from the project or program.

In many developing countries, such as the Republic of Mali, which is located in the Sahel region of West Africa, many of the major development programs, especially those designed for the rural population are promoted by the central government. In general, this could be because the amount of funds required to implement such projects are huge. Most of the capital goods and services required have to be imported. The amounts run into tens of millions of dollars, most of which are required in foreign exchange and are beyond the financial means available internally to the central government or its constituent sections. These programs therefore require external funding. Direct private foreign investments in many of these developing countries, especially in many Sahel countries are not yet substantial.

UNCTAD figures on net flow of foreign direct investment into Mali showed a negative of US $6 million in 1987. It rose to a positive of US

$69.7 million in 1997.³ According to data from the World Bank published in September 2008,⁴ portfolio equity net inflows for the two periods were zero. External funding in many developing countries can only be solicited by the central governments. In 1993 terms, at $480 million, external assistance to the Republic of Mali was the equivalent of 16% of GNP and the debt burden was 100% of GNP. Official development assistance, mainly from multi lateral organizations, European Union and France, was US $57.9 billion in 2000 and moved to US $107.7 billion in 2005. The balance of trade during the 1990s was a negative of around US $192 million.⁵ The central government did not therefore have adequate amount of resources to finance, on its own, many of the development programs required to contribute towards increasing growth and reducing poverty.

In developing countries, central governments decisions on the projects for which they should solicit external funds are generally influenced by several factors such as needs of the region, location, politics, and especially on which side of the political fence the population tends to be located. Other factors should include the ground work or preparation of the project by the technical team, including the assessment, by the team, of the responses the project would elicit and which may affect its implementation. These responses should be and generally are incorporated into the design of the project or programme. The final decision of the central government is often a result of political parameters which include pressures of the different competing regions of the country and competing sections of society. The force of the pressure varies depending on the political strength of the parties involved. The closeness of the parties to the top decision maker or makers or his/her major financial backer could be a measure of the strength or influence of the specific party.

Once the decisions on the choice, type and location of the project have been settled, political pressure does not cease, as parties who consider themselves aggrieved or are not satisfied with the decisions could and would continue to exert pressure in whatever other avenues they consider appropriate to try to achieve their goals. The scene is therefore set for conflicts and disputes to surface, either covertly or overtly. In addition, external funding could come with its own terms, conditions and possibly, agenda. These may also have the possibility of allowing conflict to surface.

The Moyen Bani Program under study was intended, by building a dam at Talo, to harness and control the waters of the River Bani, a tributary of the River Niger. It is located in the Republic of Mali, a landlocked country in West Africa. The Program area is located in the administrative region of Segou in the Sudano-Sahelian region of what is known as the District of San, Segou and Bla. With regard to technical preparation, at the initial stages of the Program, there was a series of preparatory studies, surveys, consultation and dialogue missions intended to formulate the Program. They were also expected to address issues including the capacity, reactions and responses of institutions, individuals and groups of individuals. These studies and missions were carried out over several years from 1980 to 1997. Did they address all the issues? Were they able to cover all aspects of the responses, including possible conflicts which may arise? Were all the issues of capacity of all the participating individuals and bodies satisfactorily considered? A feasibility study was carried out in 1988 and environmental impact studies undertaken in 1995. Many visits to the Program areas and surrounding regions were made

Figure 1.1. Map of Mali Showing Major River Basins. *Source:* Adapted from *The New York Times* on the web. Merriam-Webster's Atlas at www.merriam-webster.com/cgi-bin/nytmaps.pl?mali.

by consulting firms which carried out the studies and reviews. This is the normal preparation procedure for most projects and programs, whether financed from internal or external sources. The Moyen Bani Program, which will be discussed in greater detail later, was financed by the African Development Fund (AfDF), the soft window of the African Development Bank, the Development Fund of the Organization of Petroleum Exporting Countries (OPEC) and the Government of Mali.

As we shall see in Chapter Three, this program which had been in the making for a long time, took another six years to be completed. It was appraised in 1996 and reappraised in 1997, and then approved for funding by the board of directors of the African Development Bank in 1998. Why was the implementation delayed? This prolonged execution period was due to the time it took to resolve the conflict which arose. The conflict, like many such conflicts related to resource management in rural areas, especially irrigation projects where a dam was to be constructed, was between upstream and downstream populations. In the present case, the population upstream from the dam was from the Bla and Bani regions whereas the downstream population was from Djenne. These latter were located around one hundred and fifty kilometers from the place where the dam was to be constructed, in an area known as Talo. The crux of the conflict was the adequacy of the quantity of water, for household and economic purposes, flowing downstream of the dam. As Engel and Korf indicated, such natural resource conflicts are often very complex; the conflicts have many causes and many interconnected issues.[6] In fact, the conflict became highly politicized as one of the parties felt that the programme should not be implemented. This politicization took several forms which included the vocal protest by the Association of Natives of Djenne (AND), not those who are living regularly in Djenne, but those who were living in the capital, Bamako.[7]

Furthermore, as Susskind and Cruikshank stated, "groups unhappy with court decisions press their legislators to change the relevant laws.[8]" In the present case, it was not a court decision that the population of Djenne was not happy about, but rather about a decision by the central government. Courts would have been the very last resort for the downstream population, given the fact that judges are appointed by the central government and are not appointed for life. There were also other avenues which could have been explored before the matter was taken to the courts. The Association of Natives of Djenne therefore pressed upon one of the members of Parliament, representing Djenne to raise the issue in Parliament.[9] This raised the conflict up a notch. In addition, the conflict became externalized when an American nongovernmental organization (NGO), Cultural Survival, took up the cause of the Djenne population allegedly, for its own agenda.[10]

Before we continue further discussion on the answers to these and other questions it is important to understand some key aspects of Malian history, culture, society, administration, politics and economy. These would help us to appreciate the background to the program and the bases of this particular conflict and help us analyze it. It will also give us a better comprehension of the factors which made the Program and the ensuing conflict cost so much in terms of time and resources, both human and financial. It is expected that this will contribute to show how such a conflict can arise at different stages of a project cycle or at various stages of the relevant activities, which include project identification, preparation, appraisal, implementation, supervision, monitoring and evaluation. It would also help identify factors to monitor in such types of program and which could jeopardize inter community relations. If not identified and resolved such a situation lead to armed conflict, thus compromising security and sustainable development.

ORGANIZATION OF THE BOOK

Students of, and researchers in, project analysis, planning, design, implementation and development administration as well as those studying rural development conflicts will find the in-depth analysis worthy in their search for empirical evidence. It should also be useful to theoreticians in economic development. The analysis on the interaction of politics, conflict management and conflict resolution, on the development of the agricultural sector will prove useful for practitioners of project management. Chapter One, the Introduction, gives some of the factors considered in development decision making, especially concerning the location of programs in some developing countries. It also introduces aspects which are discussed later and which relate to the context of the conflict. These concern politics, agricultural development and conflict management and resolution in the case of the Moyen Bani Program.

Chapter Two, the Background, elaborates on the history, as well as the geography, administration, politics and economy of the country which prevailed at the time of the conception and formulation of the Program. These informed the decisions concerning the Program. These are discussed in detail inasmuch as they have a bearing on the program and the conflict. The analysis gives the factors which assist the reader in understanding how and why the conflict, which is the main subject of the book, arose and developed. This will help the reader better grasp the contours of the conflict and the dynamics considered in trying to resolve the conflict. It would also help the reader appreciate the conflict management and conflict resolution processes.

Chapter Three, the Program, discusses the Moyen Bani Program in detail, ex ante. It further examines the rationale which had been mentioned earlier, discusses the preparation stage, the process it had gone through, especially the screening processes and procedures which prevailed then in the African Development Bank. These screening processes were intended to ensure that all possible factors and responses which the Program will elicit had been factored into the design, the implementation and the disbursement sections of the Program document. The chapter goes on to explain the reasons why some of the possible responses and reactions were not considered. These include assessments and documents which should be attached to any such document submitted for funding approval by the board of directors of the AfDF. It further discusses the approval process for funding in the African Development Bank Group, during which possible responses of the implementation of the Program are anticipated and catered for. It details out the financial implications of the Program, the financiers and some of the conditions which were attached to their contributions.

Chapter Four, the Conflict, deals with the conflict, starting with definitional and theoretical aspects of conflicts, then gives the origin and major actors and protagonists of the conflict. Using such concepts and notions, as frames, perception, emotions, identity, high-context and low-context cultures, it explains the positions taken at different points in time by the different actors in the conflict. It continues with the externalization process, its major participants and the role the externalization played in the conflict, especially in the protractedness and intractability of the conflict. It discusses such aspects as conflict management, attempts at resolution, the breakthrough and final resolution. It closes with a section which wraps the whole chapter together, analyzing what went well and what did not, in the effort to resolve the six year old conflict. It analyses the development of the conflict, and the factors which played a part in the conflict. It further examines those factors which could have or should have influenced the development of the conflict. The different types, theories, perspectives and practices of conflict resolution in general, but more particularly, conflict relating to rural development are also briefly discussed. Chapter Five, the Post Conflict Period, reviews the physical implementation of the various activities of the Program. It reviews the ex post report of the investment phase of the Program and discusses the role of the different actors in the Program. It analyzes the key aspects of the Program and how the conflict affected them and how in turn, they influenced the results and outcome of the conflict.

Chapter Six, the Conclusion, summarizes the context of the Program and the development of the conflict. It reviews the different chapters and draws conclusions concerning the Program and lessons which should be learned from the analysis and which could inform the building of paradigms for project analysis, development administration, program management and conflict resolution. It draws attention to local politics and the importance they could have on local conflict. The influence which local community conflict could have on national issues and national politics in developing countries are also discussed. The lessons could help Mali and other developing countries in Africa, as they strive to address their food security problems through harnessing the waters and other viable natural resources within their borders, for irrigation and economic development purposes.

NOTES

1. Chuku-Dinka R. SPENCER "Politics, Public Administration, and Agricultural Development: A Case study of the Sierra Leone Industrial Plantation Development Program, 1964–67. *The Journal of Developing Areas.* 12(1). October 1977. pp 70, 78. Published by the Western Illinois University, Macomb, Illinois.

2. Matt SANDY, "Blair's Guru's daughter loses fight for safe seat", at Daily Mail on line 18 May 2009: http://www.dailymail.co.uk/news/article-1183455/Blair-gurus-girl-Georgia-Gould-22-loses-fight-safe-seat.html also www.Insidethegame.com/Olympics/OlympicsNews. London. 18–19 October 2009.

3. UNCTAD- www.unctad.org/sections/dite_fdistat/docs/wid_cp_ml_en.pdf.

4. World Bank Group. "Mali at a Glance." September 24, 2008. At www.worldbank.org.

5. World Bank Group. "Mali-World Development Indicators database." April 2009. At www.worldbank.org.

6. Antonia ENGEL and Benedikt KORF "Negotiation and Mediation Techniques for Natural Resource Management." Rome: Food and Agriculture Organization of the United Nations 2005, p 20.

7. ESSOR Newspaper, no. 15193 of 2004-04-27... See also www.essor.gov.ml and "Afrique au Quotidien" Article 502. SyfiaInfo, February 1, 1999.

8. Lawrence SUSSKIND and Jeffrey CRUIKSHANK "Breaking the Impasse, Consensual Approaches to Resolving Public Disputes." The MIT-HARVARD Public Disputes Program, New York: Basic Books. 1987. p 4.

9. ESSOR Newspaper, no. 15193 of 2004-04-27... see also www.essor.gov.ml.

10. The Djenne Project, Mali: Jean Louis Bourgeois, Coordinator, by Deidre d'Entremont, July 31, 2001, *Cultural Survival Quarterly.* 25(2).

Chapter Two

Background

HISTORY AND GEOGRAPHY

Mali, located in West Africa, is bordered in the west by the Republics of Mauritania, Senegal and Guinea, in the east by the Republic of Niger, in the north by the Republics of Mauritania and Algeria and in the south by the Republics of Cote d'Ivoire and Burkina Faso. It became independent of France on September 22, 1960. Its history dates back to the third century B.C/BCE. In fact, evidence has been uncovered by archaeological excavations which purport to show that an ancient town existed at the site of the town Djenne-Jeno in Mali's Inland Delta Region as early as the third century B.C/BCE.[1] The fact that the downstream area has historic significance contributed to complicating the conflict furthermore. This was exploited by the NGO and contributed to delays in the implementation of the Moyen Bani Program.

Historically, Mali existed as part of several kingdoms and empires with different rulers having different ethnic affiliations. The most renowned rulers include Soundiata Keita and Samory Toure, both of the Madingue ethnic group, Amadou Tall of Tukulor origin and others of Bamabara origin. The territories controlled by these different rulers, over time, fell to the annexing powers of the French in the latter part of the nineteenth century. The annexation process was substantially completed by 1899 and modern-day Mali could be considered as having come into existence at that time. However, France had to spend several more years trying to pacify the various ethnic groups and their leaders. For a brief history of early Mali and Colonial Mali, it would be worthwhile to read Pascal James Imperato.[2] The French ruled Mali until it obtained its independence in 1960. The French colonial administration was characterized by highly centralized decision-making. The regions were implementing policies and decisions taken at the center with varying degrees of participation of the regions. This centralized decision making was inherited by independent Mali. This fact, to a very large extent, greatly influenced development decisions in post colonial and post-independence days.

Post-independence Mali, however, could not completely ignore the regions in decision making as even military governments had to contend with the ethnic diversity of the population. Susskind and Cruikshank stated that conscientious politicians have to balance numerous considerations, and that many political decisions cross political boundaries.[3] This consideration of the regions and their views helped Mali to avoid major overt racial and ethnic strife, in spite of the diverse ethnic groups. The size of the country, 1,240,190 km^2, and the existence of low human density contributed to avoiding serious conflict over land. However, the conflict of the central government and the Tuareg, an ethnic group in the north, could be considered more of a development issue and a fight for development resources than just a conflict over land. The Tuareg want more development for their region. The need for more development for all regions was not lost on the central government over the years. This will become clearer as we go on to discuss the development options for the various regions. The violence which had erupted sporadically in the Tuareg region is evidence that there could be tension if development resources are not seen to be equitably distributed. This is very important in the analysis of the conflict related to the Moyen Bani Program. This conflict related to the development options proposed for the Bla area and which the people of Djenne believed would negatively affect their own agriculture. Both the Bla area and the Djenne area were very much affected by the drought which ravaged the Sahelian regions of Mali in the 1970s and 1980s. These seriously reduced the water potential of the Niger and its tributaries.

Mali is in the Soudano-Sahelian region, which means that the rainfall is generally very sparse. Annual average rainfall in Mali is a minimum of 45 mm and a maximum of 1500 mm, with the mean being 440 mm. It varies from 1500 mm in the south and the west, around Sikasso and Kayes, to 45 mm in the far north in Taoudeni, passing through 440 mm in the central regions around Segou. Because of this rainfall pattern, the vegetation also varies from forest in the south and west to brush land in the central region and desert conditions in the north. The volume of crop production and the types of crop grown also vary from paddy in the southern, in the western and eastern regions, to maize in the central region and cotton in the northern region. Development options, especially as they relate to agriculture, therefore have to work around, and, with the limitations imposed by the climate and the vegetation. This is so especially as moist woodland savanna around the exit of the River Niger in the Republic of Guinea gives way to progressively drier savanna and semi-desert conditions in many areas of Mali. Consequently, certain crops have to be emphasized in certain regions to achieve optimum total production levels. Production possibilities could be substantially expanded when we include the opportunities brought about by the availability of water resources.

Mali is a repository of several large tributaries of the River Niger which crosses the country from the south-west as it leaves the watershed area in the Republic of Guinea, travels through Djenne and up to the north by the ancient city of Timbuktu, through Gao, and heads south through the Republic of Niger. Tributaries such as the Bani and the Tinkisso, and the Niger itself, provide natural sources of water for the population, plants, and animals. The tributaries thus provide opportunities to harness water resources for development purposes. Mali has an area of 578,850 km^2 within the basin of River Niger. This represents 25.5% of the total area of the River Niger basin. The potential for irrigation in Mali is 0.56 million hectares and actual area under irrigation is 0.18 million hectares, which represented 33% of the potential. When the Senegal River basin is included, the potential for irrigation increases to 0.57 million hectares and the actual area under irrigation goes up to 0.19 million hectares.[4]

Harnessing the potential presented by these water resources has been an important factor for development in Mali. In colonial times, the French colonial government built and harnessed the waters of the River Niger starting with the implementation of a project to build a dam at a point between Bamako and Timbuktu in 1921. This was intended to grow cotton to reduce the dependence of France on cotton imported from the United States of America. Even though this was not as successful as was desired, the French colonial government later established the "Office du Niger," which was to build a dam in 1931 and grow both export crops such as cotton as well as food crops such as cereals, for the population. The dam was built; but the original objective of 1,000,000 acres is yet to be achieved. Nevertheless, irrigation projects are recognized as a critical means to achieve the level of development in the areas where rainfall is very scarce, given the stress caused to plants by the shortage of water. It was in continuity of harnessing the waters of the Niger and its tributaries for the development of agriculture that the Moyen Bani Program was designed.

POLITICS, ADMINISTRATION AND ECONOMICS

The preceding background information would not be complete without a brief overview of the political situation and the administrative set-up which existed at the time of the conception, planning, preparation, appraisal and implementation of the program. This would help understand the context in which the decision to promote the Moyen Bani Program was made. In 1991, the government of Moussa TRAORE, president of the Republic of Mali was overthrown by a military coup, led by Lt Colonel Amadou Toumani Toure, who led a transition government and convened a National Conference to deliberate on a new constitution for the country. He believed that the army should not be involved in running the country. Based on his belief and with possible encouragement from France, a major financial backer of governments in Mali, he then, in 1992, organized national legislative and presidential elections. In addition to France, the United States, the international community, especially the World Bank, the United Nations Financial systems, and the African Development Bank were also heavily involved in providing financial support for the Malian Republic. Under President Moussa Traore, who was a general turned civilian, the country was virtually one-party as political parties were strongly discouraged.

The post-1991 situation was a very different picture from the previous military cum one-party political scene under President Moussa Traore. In anticipation of the elections, several political parties were formed, some around ethnic groups, but many with some amount of broad national appeal. The most dominant of these latter, was the "Alliance pour la Democratie au Mali" (ADEMA). It was led by a Professor of History, Alpha Oumar Konare, who won the presidential elections in 1992, and became president for the statutory period of five year. His party was the most dominant during his term of office. He again won reelection in 1997. However, though ADEMA was the dominant party during the ten-year period of Professor Konare's term in office, the political scene was far from calm. There were many changes of Prime Ministers and many social upheavals. There were strikes, students' protests, and many breakaways and alliances among the many political parties which existed at that time. Also during this period, the Tuareg, the nomadic people of the north and east, experienced a collapse of their livestock-based economy due mainly to the drought conditions which certain parts of the country were experiencing. This caused frictions and disputes with their neighbors over natural resources and led to several instances of fighting. In many instances, outside mediation, by Libya and Algeria helped the central government to ease the tensions with the Tuaregs and thereby get on with the business of development.

Following the end of the military dictatorship and high centralization of decision making, the elected government was severely challenged in terms of administration of the various regions. During his electoral campaigns Professor Konare gave decentralization of decision making an important place in his political program. The Decentralization and Deconcentration Office ("Mission de decentralisation et deconcentration"—MDD) which he set up to ensure that decision making is devolved to the regions was attached to the ministry responsible for local government. The National Assembly adopted the "Loi Cadre" (Framework Law) on decentralization in 1993. After this, it was felt that the decentralization and the "deconcentration" were of such importance that it should be under the authority of the prime minister and head of government. This, it was felt, would enhance the implementation and facilitate the high level decision which would be necessary in any dispute between ministries and among ministerial colleagues. Professor Konare had given a pivotal role to decentralization and therefore just before the election of regional bodies, he gave instructions for the MDD to be attached to President's Office. It now became the "Mission de Décentralisation et des Réformes Institutionelles (MDRI)."

The Loi Cadre on decentralization provided for the establishment of local government authorities, each with its own elected deliberative and executive bodies. These were the communes, the districts, the regions and the district of Bamako, the capital. The powers that were to be transferred from the central government were specified in the law, as well as resources, means and assets which were to be transferred. These elected bodies however, were subjected to oversight by the central government. There was no precise statement on the hierarchical relations among the four local authorities mentioned above. The law provided for the establishment of "Haut Conseil des Collectivites Territoriales", (HCCT), the High-Level Council of Local Government Authorities. This body was empowered to advise on all issues concerning local governments. The central government is obligated to consult it on all matters relating to local governments. The HCCT cannot be dissolved. These are the provisions of the law.

It was however, in 1996, three years after the law was adopted, that Parliament passed the bill establishing six hundred and eighty-two new communes in addition to the nineteen which had previously been set up. This establishment followed a national debate which lasted over an eighteen-month period. This debate set the stage for the different criteria, legal, technical and others which were to be used to group villages together into communes. Some of these criteria include the desire to cooperate and the economic viability of the end product commune. The seven hundred and one communes replaced the previous organization of the country which was based on two hundred and forty-six "arrondissement." After the communes were put in place, in 1999, Parliament passed the bill which created districts and regions. These latter were empowered to elect their own deliberative and executive bodies. Associations were set up which grouped the different municipalities and another which grouped local authorities, districts and regions. Although the means and resources to implement the decentralization were to have been furnished at the time of the establishment of the local government authorities, Souleymane Diarra et. al.[5] write that this was not consistently done and the transfer of real authority was only gradually done over several years. In some cases this has yet to be finalized.[6]

It was against this background of student protests, proliferation of political parties, intense political activity and ongoing administrative reform that the Moyen Bani Programme was taking shape. This Programme had once been considered during the French Colonial period as deserving of attention.[7] The Programme was resuscitated, given the decreasing trend in agricultural production noted above, which was due to among others, the long periods of drought in the 1970s and 1980s. The decreasing trend in agricultural production, especially cereals, forced the central government to have recourse to large amounts of food imports. Import of food which was US $64 million in 1987 jumped to US $111 million in 1997, an increase of 73%. Total import bill moved from US $479 million to US $753 million during the same period, representing an increase of 57%. Total exports during the same period were US $256 million and US $561 million respectively.[8] This was costing the country huge sums of money, especially foreign exchange, of which the country did not and still does not have in satisfactory amounts. In fact, at the time, agricultural exports were the country's main source of foreign exchange and agriculture was the mainstay of the economy. In 1998, agriculture accounted for around 49% of GDP and around 80% of the active labor force.[9] In such a situation, the unfavorable agricultural economy was forcing a downward trend on the general economy. Export of goods and services compared with imports showed a net negative balance of US $319 million in 1987. This dropped to a net negative of US $263 million in 1997. Total outstanding debt for the same period moved 54% from US $2.05 billion to US $3.15 billion. Debt service moved 23% to US $85 million a year.[10] The production of cereals as well as the area harvested fluctuated downward over the period 1990 to 2000 as can be seen in Table 2.1.

Table 2.1 is better illustrated by the graph in Figure 2.1.

Table 2.2 can be illustrated in the graph in Figure 2.2.

In the absence of widespread irrigation schemes, production was greatly dependent on rainfall and this was erratic over the years. Table 2.2 shows the total production of the major cereals. Despite the focus on cereals, cotton was the main export crop of Mali. It was the largest exporter in Africa, with 261 000 tonnes in 2003/2004.[11] The international price of cotton was falling sharply; the FAO world Cotlook "A" index moved from 151 US cents in 2003/4 to 115 US cents in 2004/5. This decline was aided by higher

Table 2.1. Statistics on Cereals-Areas Harvested in Hundred Thousand Hectares

Cereals	1990	1991	1992	1993	1994	1995	1996	1997	1998	1999	2000
Fonio	0.477	0.560	0.312	0.395	0.545	0.458	0.244	0.237	0.300	0.340	0.230
Maize	0.170	1.857	1.916	2.569	2.842	2.054	1.857	2.024	2.300	2.600	1.40
Millet	12.133	10.747	9.938	1.318	14.04	12.855	9.357	8.789	9.5	11.5	10.50
Rice paddy	8.087	7.066	8.886	10.325	9.766	8.510	5.412	5.717	6.8	7.2	6.0
Sorghum	8.087	7.066	8.886	10.325	9.766	8.510	5.412	5.717	6.8	7.2	6.0
Wheat	0.001	0.002	0.001	0.001	0.002	0.003	0.002	0.002	0.004	0.007	0.005
Total	24.380	22.877	23.398	28.947	30.051	26.936	20.166	20.095	22.240	25.208	21.483

Adapted from MALI-Agricultural Bulletin

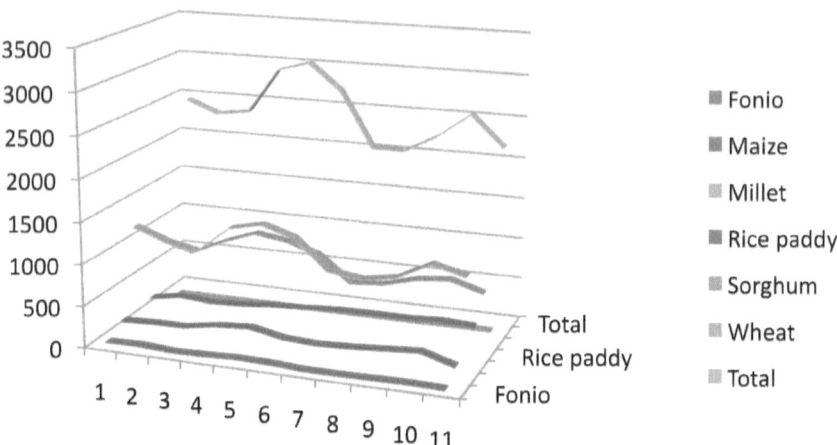

Figure 2.1. Fluctuations in Area Harvested in Cereals- 1990–2000.

expectation of supply compared with demand and also by trade distorting interventions in the form of government support provided to their exporters by developed countries such as USA and France as well as by some emerging countries, such as China.[12] The funds from export were estimated at around US $590 million f.o.b in 1998, and the import amount was around US $600 million, c.i.f for the same period.[13] The funds from export were therefore far from adequate to support all the foreign exchange needs of the development activities in the country.

Estimated budgeted revenue in 1997 was $40 million less than the expenditure for the same period which was $770 million, of which capital expenditure was $30 million.[14] In a bid to help redress the decline in revenue

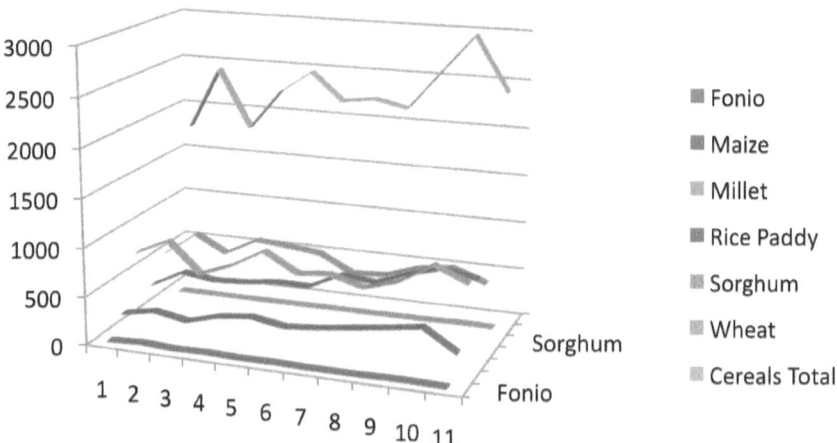

Figure 2.2. Fluctuations in Cereal Production- 1990–2000.

Table 2.2. Statistics on Cereal—Production in Million Metric Tonnes

Cereals	1990	1991	1992	1993	1994	1995	1996	1997	1998	1999	2000
Fonio	0.022	0.041	0.021	0.03		0.022	0.015	0.015	0.020	0.023	0.014
Maize	0.197	0.257	0.193	0.283		0.265	0.294	0.342	0.387	0.438	0.223
Millet	0.737	0.890	0.582	0.708		0.707	0.739	0.641	0.746	0.953	0.803
Rice paddy	0.282	0.454	0.410	0.428		0.463	0.627	0.589	0.718	0.810	0.745
Sorghum	0.531	0.770	0.602	0.777		0.710	0.541	0.559	0.674	0.714	0.592
Wheat	0.002	0.003	0.001	0.002		0.006	0.003	0.003	0.007	0.015	0.010
Total	1.72	2.41	1.81	2.23		2.17	2.22	2.15	2.55	2.95	2.39

Source: Adapted from: Mali—Agricultural Bulletin Board

and address the financial situation in the country, some of the developed countries and international financial institutions, had been, since 1992, supporting, different structural adjustment programmes in Mali. Some progress was made in reducing some financial imbalances; however, the level of the internal resources could not yet permit the government to cover expenditures relating to all public capital investments. Internal investment increased from 22% to 26% of gross domestic product from 1993 to 1996; gross savings, marginally increased only from 6% to 11% of gross domestic product.[15] Government, therefore, instituted a new economic and financial programme of which the major objective was to strengthen the mobilization of internal resources. This would contribute toward reducing the dependence on external aid.

The Moyen Bani Program was one of the programs the government was considering to harness and control the waters of various tributaries of the River Niger in a bid to reverse the downward trend in the production of some agricultural products. In turn, this would help the finances of the country. In the Bla, Segou, and San area, where the programme was to be located, the waters of the River Bani were receding. Some of the economic activities which were possible in times of full water levels became impossible to continue under the new hydrological regime which followed the droughts of past years. These included full crop immersion irrigation method and fishing. The project cycle for the Moyen Bani Program which started in the 1980s, was accelerated in 1994 following the increasingly deteriorating situation caused by the droughts and after the feasibility studies which were carried out in 1988. An environmental impact study was undertaken in 1995 on the initiative of the African Development Bank. Because of the absence of more recent topographic data, this study could not precisely evaluate the influence of the flood levels and risks of inundation of some villages located at the downstream of the dam.

How did the lack of this information affect the development of the program? Was there any validity in the protests by the downstream population? How did the government react to the protest initially? Was there any justification in the externalization of the protest and the ensuing conflict or was it just a matter of interference by the NGO, in furtherance of its political agenda? What effect did the protest and the NGO's action have on the way the conflict developed? What influence did the fact that the major financier of the project was an international development bank with strong and very vocal shareholding by the developed countries of North America and Western Europe, have on the way the conflict was eventually resolved? What were the issues involved? Who were the parties involved? The chapters which follow will address these issues and look at how the conflict was managed and finally resolved. They will also address the consequences of the conflict and analyze the background of the Program. The book is intended to contribute to the discussions on the different dimensions of project analysis, project planning, development administration and the study of conflict resolution in rural development programs. It is hoped that it will assist to put in place, ex ante, measures to smooth the bumps in the implementation of projects. This will contribute to the chances of development programs and projects meeting their objectives, realizing the expected outcomes and having the expected impact.

NOTES

1. Pascal James IMPERATO, "Mali. A Search for Direction." Boulder and San Francisco, Dartmouth and London. Westview Press. 1989. Page 15.
2. Pascal James IMPERATO, "Mali. A Search for Direction." Boulder and San Francisco, Dartmouth and London. Westview Press. 1989. Page 15.
3. Lawrence SUSSKIND and Jeffery CRUIKSHANK- "Breaking the Impasse. Consensual Approaches to Resolving Public Disputes." New York: Basic Books. 1987. Page 9.
4. "Irrigation Potential in Africa: A Basin Approach." Land and Water Bulletin No.4. Rome. FAO. 1997.
5. Souleymane DIARA et al "Decentralization in Mali: Putting Politics into Practice." Bulletin # 362, SNV Mali. Amsterdam. Royal Tropical Institute (KIT)- KIT Development, Policy and Practice.
6. Souleymane DIARA et al "Decentralization in Mali: Putting Politics into Practice." Bulletin # 362, SNV Mali. Amsterdam. Royal Tropical Institute (KIT)- KIT Development, Policy and Practice. p 39.
7. Applet-Magic.com-Office du Niger and the Scheme to Irrigate the Sahara Desert" www.sjsu.edu/faculty/watkins/officeduniger.htm.
8. World Bank Group –"Mali at a Glance." September 24, 2008. At www.worldbank.org.
9. "Mali Economy" in www.geographic.org and www.photius.com/wfb199/mali/mali_economy.html.
10. World Bank Group—"Mali at a Glance." September 24 2008. At www.worldbank.org.
11. FAO. "Cotton Commodity Notes." www.fao.org/es/esc/en.15/304/highlight_307.html.
12. WTO- Report of the African Regional Workshop on Cotton, Cotonou, Republic of Benin—March 23–24, 2004.- Also: "Fairtrade Foundation report reveals $47 billion subsidies locking West African Farmers in Poverty." At: www.fairtrade.org.uk/press_office/press_releases_and_statements/november/fairtrade_foundation_report_reveals_47_billion_subsidies_locking_west_african_farmers_in_poverty.aspx.

13. "Mali Economy" in www.geographic.org and www.photius.com/wfb199/mali/mali_economy.html.

14. "Mali Economy" in www.geographic.org and www.photius.com/wfb199/mali/mali_economy.html.

15. IMF—Mali: Selected Economic and Financial Indicators, 1994–2001. At www.imf.org.

Chapter Three

The Program[1]

RATIONALE

Agricultural production in Mali was and is greatly dependent on rainfall. Many areas, especially the area under consideration in the Segou, San, and Bla districts, were severely affected by the droughts of the 1970s and 1980s. It was also noted earlier that harnessing the waters of the Niger and its tributaries would considerably reduce the impact of the erratic rainfall on agricultural production. However, the drought had also seriously reduced the levels of the River Niger and its tributaries. The rate of flow of these water bodies in those districts, did not allow the overflow to be of the levels required for local farmers to practise complete flood cultivation agriculture such as was done in the years prior to the drought. Consequently, the plains where this type of agriculture was practised were abandoned. Some of the population left the region whereas others had to settle for cultivating rain-fed crops with all the risks involved and for which productivity was very low. Yields for rain-fed rice cultivation were around 1 ton per hectare, whereas yields for irrigated rice cultivation, were between 2.8 and 3.4 tons per hectare.[2] (WARDA-Overview of Rice in Africa, Somado et al). As discussed in Chapter One, the various governments since the 1980s were cognizant of the situation in the region and the problem of rural exodus. The technology existed to harness the River Bani, a tributary of the River Niger, and to restore the flood plains to levels which would permit the cultivation of agriculture throughout the year.

The harnessing of the waters of the River Bani would make it possible for farmers to return to their abandoned lands and contribute to the production of food and other crops. All of this would have a salutary effect on the economy, with consequent positive impact on the income and wellbeing of the population. The government which would succeed in achieving this goal would thus have demonstrated its concern for the people and in the process would acquire much needed support from the population. It would also acquire much needed votes and most probably extend its stay in office. As discussed earlier the period of mid 1990s was one of serious social discontent and protests. There was therefore a sense of urgency both in addressing the hemorrhaging of scarce foreign exchange used to import large quantities of food for the population and in showing that the government was concerned about the well-being of the rural population. This show of concern and the reduction in the food import expenditure could act as a counterbalance to the protests and strikes, which were mainly concentrated in the urban areas. These were the areas from which the various governments had garnered most of their earlier support. For the government, the Moyen Bani Program, which was to be carried out in two phases, would have contributed to restoring some faith in its ability to seriously address the diminishing trend in the economy of which the decline in the agricultural economy was a contributory factor.

Was it then only a political motivation or was there a genuine desire on the part of the government to improve the well-being of the population, starting with those in severe distress situation in the districts of Segou, San, and Bla? In fact, given the seriousness of the economic situation in the districts and their earlier importance to food production, which accounted for a good portion of the cereal supply of the country, it could be safely argued that there was genuineness to address the decline in the Moyen Bani region. In addition, as mentioned in Chapter Two, the French Colonial Administration had given serious thought to developing a program in the area. Although it had been under consideration for some time, (i.e. since the early 1980), the Moyen Bani Program received its formal induction into the project cycle of the AfDB with a visit of a mission by the African Development Bank in 1989. The mission was charged to formally identify the major contours of the Program, and to assess possible areas of concern, possible responses, outcomes and impacts. Prior to this mission, the Bank had financed a detailed feasibility study which was finalized in 1988, and which made possible the identification mission of 1989.

PREPARATION AND APPRAISAL

From the feasibility study and the identification stages, and after discussions within the AfDB and the Government of the Republic of Mali, the Program passed the screening process and moved to the stage where the detailed program formulation was to be carried out. In the African Development Bank, the preparation stage is very important as this is the stage where the details of the program are crafted and the design formulated. It is at this stage that the responses which the program will elicit are identified and evaluated; the capacity of the institutions are assessed and appropriate measures to mitigate or nullify any negative probabilities are incorporated in the detailed design of the program. Were these aspects satisfactorily considered and prepared for in the Moyen Bani Program? Did the preparation team envisage the possibility of any conflict at all? Was the preparation team equipped to address the various concerns and responses which the program would elicit, in terms of specialties in the mission composition and the amount of time allowed for the task? What factors influenced the mission composition and duration?

The composition of the preparation teams was defined in the Operations Manual which guides all operational activities. It was also a function of the specific nature of the project, its objectives, results, outcome and expected impact. Composition, however, could and were also influenced at times, by budget considerations, especially the adequacy of the budget allocation and the specific timing of the mission in the budget cycle. It was also influenced by the actions and activities planned in the project. Another factor taken into consideration was the completeness of the feasibility and other studies which had been carried out. Completeness in turn, was a factor of the composition of the team which prepared the studies. In the case of the Moyen Bani Program, the Consulting Firm which carried out the Study in 1988 had the composition relevant for the technical and economic feasibility of the proposed civil work for the control of the water level. Among others, these included agronomists, irrigation engineers, water engineers, socio-economists, agricultural economists and economists.[3] The environmental aspects were yet to be examined.

The AfDB preparation team which carried out the field mission had similar composition as indicated for the consulting firm. In addition, it included a financial analyst and an environmental specialist. In carrying out its field mission, the preparation mission, met with and discussed the program with all the parties involved, who were slated to be involved and those likely to be involved in its implementation. These included government officials, private sector individuals and organizations as well as representatives of non-governmental organizations. They also met with village associations and community- and farmer-based organizations. These meetings were intended to contribute towards finalizing the detailed design and parameters of the Program. They were also intended to assess the capacity of those to be involved in the Program and to anticipate the responses the Program would elicit.

Outside of the Republic of Mali, the team met with officials of the Niger Basin Authority, based in Niamey, Republic of Niger. This organization seeks to foster cooperation in the management and development of the resources of the River Niger. Following the various missions at the preparation stage, an environmental impact study was carried out. This study was finalized in 1995. This study looked at the impact on the physical aspects, and also considered the sociological and societal impacts. The need for a more detailed environmental impact study with more recent data might have been missed out in the earlier screening process at the identification stage. The company selected according to AfDB procedure to carry out the feasibility study was non-African. Did that influence the design and formulation of the Program with respect to the perception of the sociological and cultural features of the peoples of the specific region in Mali? Even though, to a large extent, sociological and cultural aspects could be considered as location-specific, Africans do not necessarily have a monopoly of knowledge on them. We therefore do not necessarily expect any contention on these aspects, although perception of possible conflict areas may vary depending on, among others, the original culture of the perceiver. These aspects actually later became issues in both the conflict and the conflict resolution processes and effort.

In the AfDB, preparation reports are examined by an internal working group composed of multi-disciplinary specialists, who assess whether the project or program has taken into consideration in its design all the responses which the project or program will elicit. The group also assesses the capacity of the organizations and institutions which will be involved in the implementation of the program. It was during the review at this stage that the group noticed that the environmental impact study did not contain satisfactorily precise data on the levels of the overflow of the River Bani and the risks of flooding it could cause to some of the villages upstream and downstream. This was mainly due to the absence of precise recent topographical data. An appraisal team carried out a field mission in 1996. It was during this field mission that the team found that additional studies were required to fully capture the aspects which the team felt were critical to the design and implementation of the Program. These initial complementary studies concerned the optimization of the dam to be located in Talo in the basin of the River Bani. They also concerned in-depth analysis and studies for hydrological, topographical, environmental and socio-economic aspects. These studies were completed in 1997. The initial additional studies which were carried out enabled the government and the AfDB to conclude that the dam would not amplify the risks of flooding in the villages which are upstream and downstream. Even though this may be so, the issue of whether there would be enough water for the downstream population did not seem to have been specifically mentioned.

Before it is considered as final, the appraisal report goes through various rigorous screening processes. These are expected to ensure that all possible responses have been covered in the analysis and the capacity of all institutions and individuals to participate satisfactorily in project implementation has been scrutinized. So it was for the Moyen Bani Program. The screening process included an internal working group review meeting. If this level is passed satisfactorily, the document is taken to the level of interdepartmental working group review meeting. This latter group is composed of multi disciplinary specialists from various departments involved in the project or which will be called upon to participate in its supervision. Specialists review every aspect of the program and cover all possible responses that the program could elicit. These include macro-economic, financial, legal, environmental, disbursement, socio-economic as well as procurement issues. It would thus be appropriate to expect that potential conflicts which could possibly arise and possible options for resolution would have been discussed.

In fact, the appraisal document contains a section which specifies the negative and positive effects of the program and measures to mitigate or eliminate the negative aspects. These measures should have been included in the design of the final program document to be presented for final approval and for approval of funding. The fact that it was at the appraisal stage at which it was recommended that additional studies were to be carried out indicated omissions at the previous review stages. This made it critical to examine the earlier results of the prior review stages to ensure that all possible responses, capacities and contingencies were adequately addressed in the design.

Such a critical review was carried out prior to presentation for funding approval. Funding approval was and is the responsibility and prerogative of the board of executive directors. The board of directors represents the shareholders of the AfDB. It is composed of twelve members representing the fifty-three African countries, grouped together as regional members. The board also has six members representing shareholding countries which are not physically located on the African continent. These are mainly countries from western and northern Europe, the United States, Canada and some countries in Asia, including Japan, Saudi Arabia, Kuwait, India and China. Other shareholding countries are from South America and they are Argentina and Brazil. These non-African countries are generally known as "non regional" members. The board members and their staff have oversight on the contents and completeness of the document presented to them for funding approval. Board members can therefore request additions, more information and details and modification to the design of the project and program.

In this way, it is expected that all possible issues relating to responses, capacity and contingency would have been addressed before funding is approved. As the Moyen Bani Program was financed under the soft window, AfDF, the composition is different, with majority of the Board members representing non regional countries. As the AfDF is almost entirely financed by the non regional participating countries, they have the final say on all matters which concern the AfDF, including project or program funding. The Moyen Bani Program was therefore discussed and approved by the board of directors of the AfDF.

Like all institutions where different countries make up the membership, politics, especially the politics of the countries represented in the board, can play a significant or an insignificant role. As has been seen earlier, Mali had come out of a long period of more than twenty-three years of military rule, then one party dictatorship. The coup d'état of 1991 and the restoration of democracy and elections in 1992 ensured that the country had a lot of international goodwill. This was enhanced by a professor of history turned president who advocated the rule of law and democratic principles. In addition, the new policy of the government supported a disengagement of government from the productive sectors and obligated the producers and other economic actors to adapt to the liberal economic exigencies based on private sector initiative. This rang a very pleasant note in the capitals of many of the board members, especially those representing Western European and North American countries. It was recognized in many of these capitals that Mali should be given all the assistance it required to further enhance democratic principles. The Moyen Bani Program was thus a very welcome way to assist the Malian population, especially the rural population.

Going back into the history of the AfDB, such support can be contrasted with the rejection in 1979 of a project promoted by the government of Equatorial Guinea to develop cocoa plantations in the country. Leaving aside the merits or demerits of the project, it must be noted that Equatorial Guinea was at that time, run by the late dictator, Mathias Nguema, in an apparently harsh and allegedly corrupt manner, with little or no civil liberties. At that time, the AfDB did not have non-regional members as it now has. Its board of directors was composed of entirely regional members, whereas the AfDF was and still is dominated by non-regional members. The Equatorial Guinea Cocoa Plantation Project was presented to the AfDF board for funding. After several hours of discussion on the merits and demerits of the project, the AfDF board of directors declined funding the project. It might have been felt that the project was going in some way to support an unpopular regime. The project was presented for funding to the board of directors of the AfDB and the funding was approved, under the then very onerous statutory terms of the AfDB. These were, and still are, much more onerous than if the AfDF board had approved the funding. It might have been felt by the Equato-Guineans, at that time, that there was a sentiment of interference. This sentiment echoed the fears held, in the late 1970s and 1980s, by some leaders of African countries about opening up the capital of AfDB to non-regional countries, mentioned by Mingst.[4]

One can see therefore, that in some ways, the tenor of the government in the country where the project is to be implemented may have some influence on the final funding decision. Unpopular governments in Africa had difficulties getting their projects approved by boards of directors of international development finance institutions, especially as the major shareholders of the major institutions are the same and are mainly from developed countries in Western Europe and North America. The African Development Bank is no different. The government of the late General Sani Abacha, head of state of Nigeria, from 1993 to1998 was generally accused by the international community of alleged corruption and such anti-democratic actions as the imprisonment of political opponents and those who criticize the regime. The Nobel Literature laureate Wole Soyinka and the world renowned musician, the late Fela Anikulapo-Kuti were put in prison by General Abacha. As such, it could be argued that it developed a lot of ill-will from many countries including those in Western Europe and North America.

Consequently, it could be argued that projects from governments not having general international goodwill might have difficulties in receiving funding approvals from international development finance institutions. In the past, such ill-will would have been very overt. However, it later became very covert and extremely subtle. What then did the AfDF board of directors approve in 1998? What were the contents of this Program that started in the late 1980s, approved for funding in 1998, which brought about a seemingly intractable conflict, and which was finally brought to some kind of fruition in 2004 and implemented until 2007?

PROGRAM AREA

Before we discuss the contents of the program, it is important to discuss the project area briefly. This will help us better to understand and analyze the conflict and why it arose. The Program was located in the administrative regions of Bla and of Segou, in the districts of San, Segou, and Bla which are within the delta zone of the tributary of the River Niger. Over the years, it was observed that in many areas, the water was drying up, especially in the Moyen Bani River, which was the only source of irrigation water in the Program area. The 1994 estimated population of the Program area was 63,700 and the dominant ethnic group was Bamabara; there were also Peulhs, Niankas, Bozos and Bobos, all of whom lived peaceably together. The major activity which occupied the population was agriculture. Market gardening, trading, livestock and fishing are secondary activities. Sixty-five rural villages were directly concerned with the Program, especially with the civil work component. These were situated in the plains of Tounga, Western, and Eastern San regions. The Program area also included some sections of the town of San which were considered rural. A large portion of the population was and is considered to be and very poor, cereal-deficit. Many had emigrated from this region to other parts of the country in a bid to eke out a living and make ends meet. The major beneficiaries of the first phase of the Program were expected to be primarily, the 1600 farmers who would be installed in the developed areas. In total, 41,000 persons were expected to benefit directly from the Program in the form of supplementary incomes.

Land tenure laws were and are very diverse in Mali. There is a cohabitation of customary and modern tenure laws inherited from the French, known as "code domanial et foncier." According to the existing legislation, the State is the owner of all the land. Villagers only have usufruct rights of their parcels of land. In the project area, the traditional land tenure predominates and the land is collectively "owned" by the extended family. It was expected that these people will continue to enjoy the usufruct of their land after the land development activities were finalized. Management of the developed land would be the responsibility of the decentralized community bodies. The map in Figure 3.1 indicates the program area.

Was the choice of the Program area appropriate and justified? From the preceding discussion, the area was in dire need of development, however, so were other areas. Was there any political motivation in the choice? As part of their mandate, governments should develop the different regions and improve the well-being of the various ethnic groups which make up the population. Thus, it can be stated that the choice of any area was within the "terms of reference" of the central government. In that regard, it can be argued that all decisions to develop any area do have political undertones. Records from the period of the French administration however, indicated that the positioning of the dam/water regulatory structure in the Talo area of the Moyen Bani was the most technically and economically justified. It was, topographically, the narrowest point on the river.[5]

PROGRAM DETAILS

In this section, we shall discuss the Program on an "ex ante" basis, before the dam was constructed. The sector goal in the appraisal report was, "to contribute to the realization of food security in the country", through the development of the plains around the middle section of the Bani River. The objectives of the overall Program which was to be implemented over a ten-year period, was to increase agricultural production. It envisaged the irrigated cultiva-

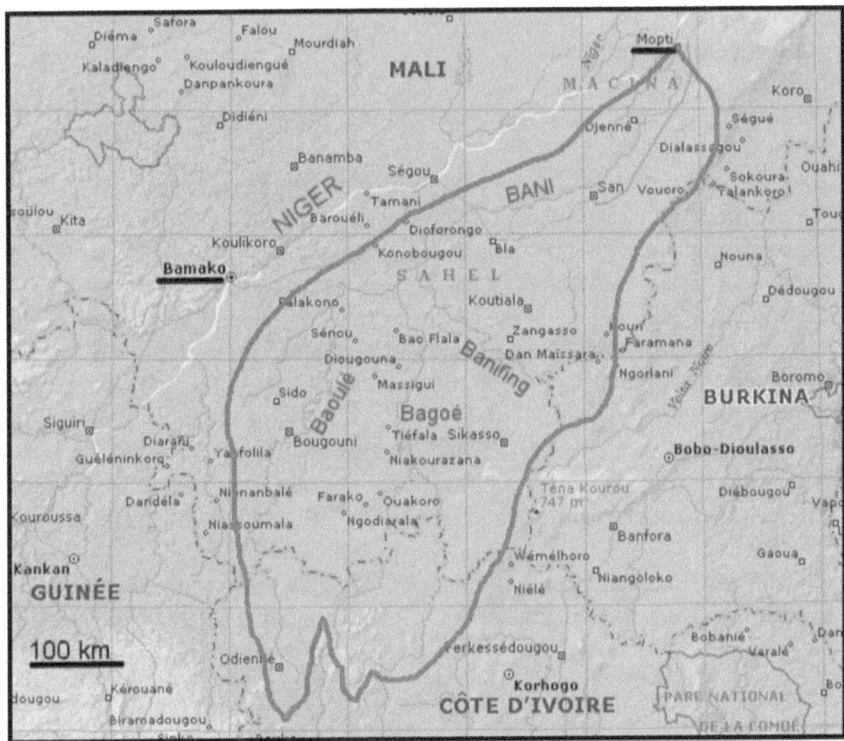

Figure 3.1. Map of Programme Area. *Source*: Adapted from Appraisal Report "Moyen Bani Program" African Development Bank.

tion under controlled flooding method of a total net area of 20,320 hectares of which 16,030 hectares would be for rice and 4290 hectares would be for aquatic fodder crop known as "borgou." The fodder crop would contribute to the development of cattle rearing. The area also included the development of 490 hectares of pisciculture ponds. Other objectives included the restoration of the environment, the rational management of the water resources and the appreciable improvement of the living standard of the population in the Program area.

What then were the activities that were going to contribute appreciably and lead to the improvement of the living standards of the population of the districts of Segou, San, and Bla? The components of the first phase of the Moyen Bani Program were as listed below.

- Hydro-agricultural land development and irrigation civil works;
- Agricultural and rural Development;
- Extension activities and accompanying measures;

- Development of activities for women;
- Programme management.

The major physical realizations of the Program were the following

- Dam at Talo with lateral dykes and principal capture canal;
- Civil works which would enable the irrigation of 7850 hectares, composed of lead canals, distribution canals, draining canals, protection dykes, dykes which separate the different plots, dykes permitting movement around the developed area.
- The rehabilitation of the Cinzanna-Talo-Katiena track measuring 46 kilometers to improve access within the area located on the left bank of the upstream area;
- The division and distribution of the developed area into plots of 2.8 hectares, settling and equipping 1,600 farmers, the cultivation of 4,750 hectares of rice, 2,470 hectares of aquatic livestock fodder and 380 hectares of fishing ponds;
- The development and cultivation of 350 hectares under complete and controlled immersion, 250 hectares in upstream, and 100 hectares downstream;

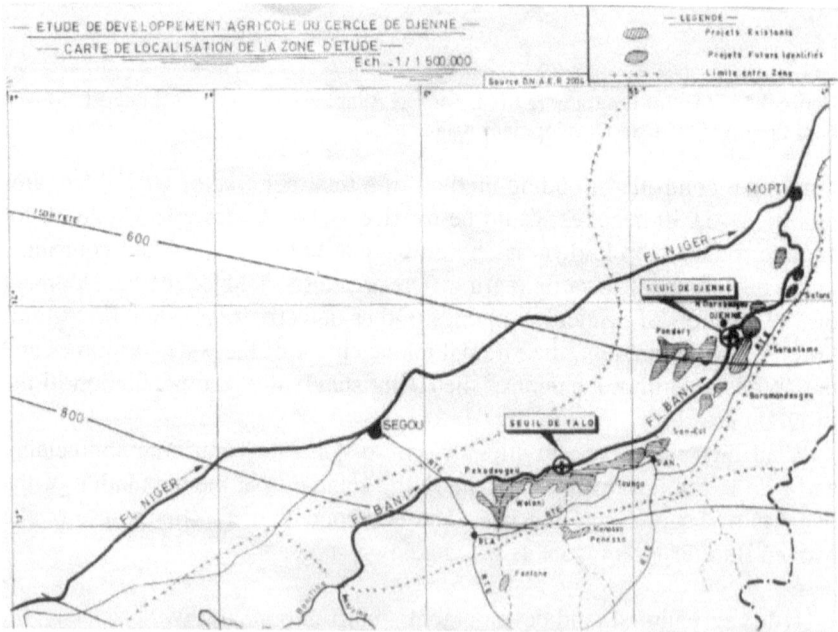

Figure 3.2. Map of Localization of Talo and Djenne Dam. *Source*: Appraisal Report "Moyen Bani Program." African Development Bank.

- The training and organization of farmers, and specific activities which would benefit women; these activities would be decided upon in a participatory manner with the women concerned;
- Village afforestation on 150 hectares, construction of drinking ponds for livestock, such activities relating to public health as training of personnel, and construction of health posts.

From a review of the different components, it would be difficult to identify one which could be considered objectionable. The dimensions of some of them could be called into question, depending on the precise objective of the person or persons querying them. Should there be wider tracks, longer tracks, the possibility of release of more or less water, increased height of the dam, the possibility of larger expanse of land to be developed, should there be more health centers? These are possibilities which could be the subjects of debate. The Program however, was more than just the physical structures. There were components relating to training, assisting in organizing the farmers, fisher folks, pastoral communities, group formation and group training, access to funds for farm development, fisheries development, and afforestation activities, provision of health facilities. These enabling activities would have ripple effects on the region and beyond, especially the rehabilitation and upgrading of tracks. The cost of all the Program activities could also be called to question. It would therefore be appropriate to review the financial aspects, including the cost of the different components.

PROGRAM COST AND FINANCIAL ASPECTS

For government-sponsored development programs, international financial institutions did not generally include taxes and duties, which are ultimately owed to the same government sponsoring the program, in the cost estimates. The total estimated cost excluding taxes and duties, but including provision for physical and price contingency of the first phase of the Program amounted to CFAF 22,173 millions (US $38.99 million). Of this, CFAF 15,243 million (US $26.81 million) were to be in foreign exchange and CFAF 6,930 million (US $12.18 million) in local currency. The major cost component was the hydro-agricultural land development and irrigation civil works. At CFAF 14,730 million (US $25.9 million), it represented 66% of the total cost of the whole first phase of the Moyen Bani Program. Under this heading, the category with the highest cost was the civil works or structures, which at CFAF 14,989 million (US $26.36

million), represented 67% of the total cost by category. These all go to show the high level of importance of the project in terms of cost to the government. In fact, the amount for the civil works component represented around 8% of the average national capital expenditure of all sectors for 1997 to 2005.[6] For these years, between 70% and 76% of the national capital expenditure were from external sources. The foreign exchange portion of the total cost of the Program represented 69%. With the growing difficulty encountered in the agricultural economy, the central government could therefore ill afford to provide that kind of foreign exchange and even the entire local currency portion over the five-year period of the first phase of the Moyen Bani Program. Were these costs too high or exorbitant to warrant any accusation of being too costly?

In a Comparative Irrigation Cost Study comparing projects in Sub-Saharan (SSA) with other developing regions by the International Water Management Institute (IWMI) published by the Consultative Group on International Agricultural Research (CGIAR) in 2007, irrigation costs in SSA are discussed in detail. It is indicated that a review of the World Bank experience between 1950 and 2003 suggested that cost per hectare for all sample irrigation projects in SSA, at 2000 prices, was between US $8,000 (hardware costs only) and US $12,000 (total cost). The cost per hectare of new construction projects was as high as US $14,000 and rehabilitation projects cost per hectare was around US $8,000. The all-sample cost figures were around seven times that in South Asia at around US $1,500 and US $1,800 per hectare respectively.

Subsequent reviews and surveys however, have cast doubts as to whether there is any evidence, in the two subsequent decades, that irrigation costs per hectare in SSA are any higher than those in South Asia. In fact, with the implementation of new schemes as opposed to rehabilitating existing ones, and with the execution of reforms and the shift from large to small scale, sample projects costs per hectare have gone down significantly. The improved forecasting of cost, improved feasibility studies and increased competition among contractors may have contributed to a decline in cost per hectare. In the case of the Moyen Bani Programme, the total cost was US $38.99 million. If we calculate the cost per hectare based on the first phase hectarage and use the total cost figure, this amounts to US $4,967. This figure however, includes components and activities such as, guarantee fund, establishment of farmer organization, group formation, and farmer and personnel training, among others.

Calculations based only on the cost of the irrigation works and equipment plus the relevant contingency (US $22.12 million), that is considering only the hardware costs, the figure drops to US $4,088 per hectare. It can thus be seen that the irrigation works constitute a significant portion of total cost. These costs per hectare were well below the amounts recorded in the CGIAR Study for earlier periods. When we calculate the cost per direct beneficiary using the total cost in the first phase, the program would cost US $24,000 per direct beneficiary and US $951 per direct and indirect beneficiary. These costs, it could be argued, were not exorbitant.

Through the construction of a water control structure at Talo, the Program was expected to encourage the flooding of the adjacent plains. This condition used to be naturally arrived at in previous decades when rainfall was abundant and regular. The technology proposed to the farmers was expected to be uncomplicated and it was envisaged that they would use simple, previously well-rehearsed, farming methods. Even though it can be argued that the cost per hectare was not phenomenal, the total amount required was still very large to be accommodated within the normal investment budget of the Malian government. The dam to be constructed in the Talo area could be considered a small- to medium-sized structure, as compared with those mentioned later. The crest length would measure 700 meters; the central portion over which the water would be flowing, that is the spillway, would measure 276 meters wide. No indication was given as to the height. But it would be safe to believe that it would not be up to the 150 meters required for classification as a large dam. This can be compared with the Manantali Dam, also in Mali, which measures almost one kilometer wide. The Kanji dam in Nigeria is nine kilometers.

Because of the costs involved, especially the foreign exchange costs, it was necessary to solicit funds from external sources. The requests were therefore made to the African Development Fund and the Development Fund of the Petroleum Exporting Countries (OPEC Fund). Table 3.1 gives the summary

Table 3.1. Summary of the Estimated Cost of the First Phase by Component

Components	Foreign Exchange	Local Currency	Total	Foreign Exchange	Local Currency	Total	% of Total
	In Thousand Million FCFA			In Million of US$			
Hydro-agricultural civil works	10.436	4.294	14.730	18.34	7.35	25.9	66.42
Agricultural & Rural Development	0.092	0.149	0.241	0.16	0.26	0.42	1.08
Extension & Accompanying measures	0.445	0.106	0.551	0.78	0.19	0.97	2.49

of the total cost of the Program per component in both foreign exchange and local currency.

The Program was therefore financed by the African Development Fund, the OPEC Fund and the Government of Mali. The contribution of the AfDF was CFAF 16,303.55 million (US $28.66 million). This represented around 73% of the total cost of the first phase of the Program, some of which were in foreign exchange (79%) and a smaller proportion in local currency. The OPEC Fund was responsible for CFAF 3,627.23 million (US $6.38 million), of which US $4.50 million were in foreign exchange. The total contribution of OPEC Fund was around 16% of the total cost and 17% of the total foreign currency portion of the cost of the Program. The government did not cover any foreign currency cost. It was responsible for CFAF 2,242.14 million or US $3.94 million, which represented 7% of the total cost of the first phase of the Program. The financing plan which specifies the contributions of the different financiers is given in Table 3.2.

The largest percentage of the cost was for the hydro-agricultural civil works component, of which the construction of the structures at US $26.4, represent more than 67% of the total cost. The AfDF, by financing US $18.9 million, that is, 72% of the total cost of the structures was the financier with the highest stake in the financing package. This made the AfDF, the major financing institution to determine the procurement method for the implementation of the category. It was therefore, to the AfDF, as we shall see later, that the NGO, Cultural Survival, turned to, when it wanted the Program to be stopped. The Association of Natives of Djenne (AND) based in the capital Bamako, exerted its own pressure to see the Program on the central government in Bamako to have the Program discontinued.

Table 3.2. Summary of the Financing Plan

Components	Foreign Exchange	Local Currency	Total	Foreign Exchange	Local Currency	Total	% of Total
	In Thousand of Million of FCFA			In Million of US$			
AfDF	12.689	3.615	16.303	22.31	6.35	28.66	73.52
OPEC Fund	2.554	1.073	3.627	4.50	1.890	6.390	16.36
Government	0.00	2.242	2.242	0.00	3.94	3.94	10.12
Total	15.243	6.930	22.172	26.81	12.18	39.00	100.00

Source: Adapted from the Appraisal Report of the first phase of the Moyen Bani Program—African Development Bank

PROCUREMENT AND MANAGEMENT

The AfDF has its own rules of procedure for procurement of goods and services required for the implementation of projects under its loans or grants. These rules, through regular coordination among development finance institutions and spurred by the fact that the major international development finance institutions have almost the same shareholders, have been harmonized across institutions. Some of these shareholders of these institutions, especially those members from North American and European countries are generally very vocal. They could thus exert pressure, overt or subtle, on decisions. These rules are intended to and do instill transparency in the choice of implementers of the various categories of expenditure. The civil works category later became the source of contention, not because of issues relating to procurement which at times is the case, but because one of the responses which the Program would elicit was not satisfactorily anticipated. The method selected was through international competitive bidding. The contention surrounding the civil work category of expenditure surfaced then to haunt the management of the Program.

The Program was an integral part of the Department of Land Development and Rural Equipment of the Ministry of Rural Development and the Environment. Setting up of the management team was among the first actions undertaken very early in the life of the Program. This was done even before the funding approval was finalized. The management team was composed of a director, a specialist in land development and irrigation, a manager, an agronomist, a socio-economist, an animal scientist, an environmentalist and support staff. The socio-economist and the environmentalist were specifically included in the management team so as to constantly monitor and evaluate environmental and sociological data and aspects, both ex ante and ex post. The protests from the AND would normally fall under their purview. What then was their role, if any, in the resolution of the conflict which later ensued? Though their role in the resolution of the conflict is not documented, it was recognized that they did participate in the information and sensitization campaign.

CONDITIONS OF THE AFDF LOAN

The external financiers, the AfDF and the OPEC Fund, apart from the lending terms which are stated in the appraisal report of the First Phase of the Moyen Bani Program, also included specific conditions and assurances which the central government had to fulfill in order to fully access the funds approved. There were conditions which had to be fulfilled before the government could have access to the funds. These are known, at the time referred to, as conditions or assurances precedent to first disbursement. They are in fact the "sine qua non" for first disbursement. The other conditions are those which have to be fulfilled in course of the implementation of the Program. The conditions are reproduced in the annex of the appraisal report of the Program. However, two particular conditions are germane to the analysis of the protest and conflict which arose later.

These concern the necessity for the Borrower, (that is, the central government) to commit itself to produce a plan for the environmental monitoring of the Program before December 31, 1998. It was also required that it puts in place an epidemiological surveillance as well as all the measures necessary for the mitigation of negative effects as envisaged in the Program. This was a commitment required before first disbursement. It was carried forward also as a more tangible condition during implementation by requiring that the reports relative to the epidemiological studies and to the mitigation measures and efforts should be submitted to the external financiers before the December 31, 1998. The other condition, which was to be fulfilled during implementation, was that the Borrower should submit proof of the establishment and functioning of the local development committee, not later than December 31, 1998. The Borrower was also required to submit documents related to the regulation of pastoralist activities in the Program area. Documents concerning the modalities of managing the Talo dam, which was to be constructed under Program, were also to be submitted before December 31, 1998. These two conditions are of particular importance as they indicate concern by the promoters, financiers and government officials, for the effect the Program would have on the environment as well as on both human and animal health. They also show that there was the desire to ensure the local populations participate in the management of the structures which are to be constructed. This local committee was also required to establish a mechanism for the participatory resolution of any potential issues which could arise relating to the Talo Dam.

EXPECTED OUTCOMES

What were the expected outcomes of the first phase of the Program? These included the availability of irrigation water on a more regular basis. In fact, it was expected that through the Program, land which had not been under cultivation for more than two decades, would finally become possible to cultivate. The benefits which the Programme was expected to bring to the area included the stabilization of food production, especially cereals, fish products and livestock products. An improvement in the living standards of the population, through an increase in their incomes, was also expected to result from the Program. The farmer- and community-based organizations as well as extension personnel were to benefit from the training modules, including literacy classes. These included improved production techniques, management of farm equipments and improved knowledge of matters relating to hydraulics and water management. The village reforestation component was intended to produce, among other things, wood to be used for cooking. This was expected to have a salutary effect on the natural forest. Another benefit from the Program was the employment possibilities it would provide during Program implementation and also after the Program became operational. From the macroeconomic point of view, the Program was expected to contribute significantly to the coverage of the cereal needs of the country. It was expected that the Program would produce around 40,000 tonnes of paddy, which would translate into 26,400 tonnes of milled rice. This represented around 20% of the average cereal deficit at that time. It was also expected to ensure, in a more permanent way, food self sufficiency of the San Region.

ECONOMIC AND FINANCIAL ANALYSIS

The financial analysis based on a farm model of 2.8 hectares of rice and 2.5 hectares of rain-fed cultivation, gave a net profit of CFAF 295,800 (US $520) in the first year of production and CFAF 603,000 (US $1,060) in the year of full production. This was expected to generate monthly income of FCFA 50,000 (US $88) which compares with the minimum wage which was around FCFA 30,000 (US $53) that time. After satisfying the need for auto consumption, the farm model used showed a net commercial profit of CFAF 381,300 (US $670) at full production year. In the case of intensive livestock models, one of which included a dairy cow, and another, beef cattle, a gross profit of CFAF 393,200 (US $691) was expected. In the case of the dairy option, the appraisal report document gave a forecast that the daily remuneration would amount to CFAF 7,865 (US $14). The daily remuneration for the beef option was expected to be CFAF 3,155 (US $6). This amount could be compared to that of less than US $2 earned by the vast majority of the population in Mali.

The Program was expected to generate an internal economic rate of return (ERR) of 13%. Sensitivity analyses indicated that Program was sensitive to a reduction in benefits, as a 10% reduction dropped the ERR to 11%, while a 10% increase in investment cost gave an ERR of approximately 12%. The sensitivity analysis however, did not include a hypothesis of a delay in the start-up year of the program, which would mean a delay in first year of production and possibly an increase in the investment cost. With the wisdom of hindsight, such an analysis would have been useful to give an indication of what effect any issue or event, such as the conflict, would have had on the profitability of the program.

ENVIRONMENTAL ASSESSMENT AND MITIGATION

The Program document discussed the main points of the environmental assessment study that was carried out. This had a direct bearing on the events that delayed the start-up of the main component of the Program. This event was the conflict which arose concerning the civil work structure. The AfDB Environmental Unit classified the Program as Category One, which meant that a detailed impact assessment study had to be carried out. The Environmental Impact Assessment Study (EIAS) carried out in 1995 was not comprehensive as it was not backed by satisfactorily detailed base line studies. These would have helped to better determine the contours of the temporary lake which was to be created by the dam at Talo. The term "temporary" was appropriate as the dam was not expected to be a water retention structure, but a water flow regulatory structure. The EIAS discussed both the positive and the negative impacts of the implementation of the Program.

The major positive impact recorded, ex ante, in the study, was the expectation that the Program would recreate the conditions of natural submersion, which had existed in the past from abundant rainfall and satisfactory river flow. This would, in turn, contribute to the regeneration of the natural vegetation cover and the soil. The deposit of sediments in the flood zones and the expected use of appropriate farming techniques would contribute to the productivity of the soil. It was also expected that the land development structures would partially compensate for the effects of the drought. This was expected to have a positive effect on recharging the aquifer and the recolonization of the area by the aquatic fauna and flora. Facilities for fisheries and for aquaculture activities would be provided.[7] These positive and negative impacts will be discussed in the next paragraph. They were part of the issues of contention which Cultural Survival raised with the promoters and financiers of the Program.

It is necessary, therefore, to review and discuss the major aspects of the negative impacts. The environmental impact assessment study summary (EIAS)[8] indicated that the shortcomings of the initial environmental study were rectified with the additional study of the structure. The summary indicated that raising the water level would lead to the flooding of some upstream villages. It was expected that such flooding would recede as the distance from the structure increased to around 20 to 30 kilometers. The summary indicated that with the exception of Wori, no village would be affected by the flooding. The villagers located more upstream than Wori would not be affected more than they were in the past under natural flooding conditions. The pollution of the soil and water resources, which were another negative result of the dam, could be brought about by more intensive use of chemical factors of production. In addition, algae have been known to exist in flooded rice cultivation plots as a result of bad utilization of fertilizers.

The quality of water of the river downstream from the dam would be affected with some negative effects on the flora and fauna of the river for a substantial distance. The summary further indicated that this could result in important health issues, especially as the river water was still being used for household uses. Modifications of the upstream river system could be great, especially in the dry season. The downstream effect, however, would be negligible, as the flow of water which went through the dam structure would be at the same frequency as before the construction of the dam and before the ravages of the drought. Another negative aspect indicated in the summary was the fact the land development, using controlled flooding could limit the movement of cattle and could lead to over grazing of the available grazing areas.

These are major negative aspects which needed satisfactory corrective measures to be included in the design and/or provided for during the implementation of the Program. One of the measures, suggested to address the overgrazing was the use of harvest residue to ensure that cattle had sufficient quantities of reserve of animal feed. Cattle were to be allowed at specific times of the year to graze, under a land use management scheme which was to be agreed upon by the farmers and livestock breeders participating in the Program. The increased possibility of the incidence of bilharzias and malaria was raised as negative results of the dam. The speed of flow of the river which the water regulatory structure would bring about was expected to reduce the incidence of the diseases. In addition, the summary postulated that the increase in income which the Program was expected to generate would help the beneficiaries, who would be affected by the health issues, to develop stronger resistance to these ailments.

The EIAS indicated that there was going to be a statistical monitoring of the major endemic diseases followed by epidemiological studies. These studies were expected to be concentrated in villages considered to be most at-risk. The negative impacts associated with expected use of fertilizers and pesticides, was to be countered by emphasizing and putting in place strict conditions for the utilization of fertilizers and pesticides. At the time of the preparation of the EIAS, Mali was yet to publish a new law regulating the approval and control of agro-pharmaceutical products. Mali was expected to and did adopt the international code of the Food and Agricultural Organization of the United Nations. This is used by the members of the Inter-Governmental Committee for the Fight against Drought in the Sahel (CILSS) of which Mali is one. The Program was also expected to adopt the Integrated Pest control System, combining biological and chemical measures.

Sedimentation in the canals was expected to occur, for which the corrective measure was that the deposits should be cleared every five years. In addition, it was indicated that dikes and banks will be repaired as necessary. Dikes were to be built to protect the village of Wori, which could run the risk of being inundated. The dike measuring three kilometers in length were intended to prevent the water from going round the dam and in this way protect the habitations in the Wori area. The responsibility for the different corrective measures was either left with the relevant government departments or was to be spelt out in agreements between the farmers and the management of the Program.

Several field missions were made to Mali and the Program area during the course of the preparation of the feasibility studies, initial complementary studies, identification, preparation and appraisal of the Program. The different missions contacted over half of the 41,000 persons directly concerned by the Program. This was done during collective and individualized sessions. Some of the sessions were held in accordance with socio-economic methodological practice to ensure that women and youths, who might not normally voice their opinion in the traditional setting, were able to express their views. Is it safe therefore to assume that the issue which became the primary cause of concern of the population living downstream of the dam structure was never brought up? The issue of the amount of water that would remain for them must have been primary in their thoughts. For, in all projects and programs where a dam structure, a water diversion structure or a water control structure had to be built, the quantity and quality of the water flowing downstream of the structure had always been an issue.

In fact, the countries along the River Nile, which include Uganda, Rwanda, Kenya, Ethiopia, Sudan, and Egypt know only too well that they have to consult each other continuously and constantly any time a structure is to be put up in any of their countries. In fact, the Nile Basin Initiative was established to facilitate such consultations. In fact, under President Nasser, Egypt nearly went to war with Sudan in the 1960s, when the latter had proposed an irrigation project which Egypt felt would deprive it of considerable amounts of water. The irrigation project was later abandoned. This could cause friction and conflict among them. Mathematical models have been developed and have been agreed among them as to the amount of water that can be removed, stopped or diverted from the River. This agreement was at-risk of becoming unraveled in 2010, as the more upstream countries, Rwanda, Uganda, Kenya etc, were becoming more vocal and were questioning the colonial agreement which gave Egypt and Sudan ninety (90%) of the waters of the River Nile. Further confirmation that the issue of downstream effects of a dam is widely known could be found in an article published in the Web Atlas on Regional Integration. It was reported that in the Senegal River Basin in 2000, Senegal froze a project to revitalize the dry valleys in the north of the country, on the expression of fears by Mauritania, of the impact a diversion of the river might have had on the Senegal River.

The notion of the effects on downstream population of any dam structure was therefore well known. It would therefore be appropriate to believe that this would have been considered by the designers and formulators of the Program and also would have been raised by the downstream population. They must have received some assurance that the water regulatory structure would not seriously affect the volume of water flowing downstream from the structure. This conclusion took into consideration the fact that the situation which prevailed at that time did not allow much water to flow downstream, as the river was drying up rapidly. How then did this assurance turn into doubt, then to a protracted dispute and finally to a conflict? This may have everything to do with the way the issue was "framed", by the population of Djenne who are the main people living downstream of the structure at the consultative sessions and group discussions undertaken. The frames used by the technical teams which discussed the matter with them during the preparatory missions could also have had some influence on this. Framing is related to perceiving and Barbara Gray[9] indicated that it involves shaping, focusing and organizing the world around us, taking and weighing new information while imparting meaning and significance to elements within the "frame."

After the meetings, discussions and consultations, the technical professionals and the Djenne population therefore might have had a "common understanding" of and agreed on the risks of reduced quantity of water flowing downstream. What then made the situation change? What then was the conflict about? What then changed the "frames", the perceptions of the parties involved? Frames help define issues, shape actions, justify them and mobilize others to take action. According to Lewicki and Gray,[10] frames are not necessarily static and they can change over time, either through intentional actions or intervention. Was there any intervention on the part of a body external to the population of Djenne *resident* in Djenne or was the change purely intentional on the part of the resident Djenne population?

NOTES

1. African Development Bank. Mali. Appraisal Report of the "Moyen Bani Program." Abidjan. 1998. Also www.riob.fr/IMG/pdf/Atelir_Dakar_BANIDef.pdf.
2. E. SOMADO, R. GUEI, and N. NGUYEN "WARDA-Overview: Rice in Africa." WARDA. Bouake. Cote d'Ivoire.
3. African Development Bank- Feasibility Study. Mali. "Moyen Bani Program." Abidjan. 1998.
4. Karen A. MINGST-"Politics and the African Development Bank." Lexington, Kentucky: University Press of Kentucky. 1990.
5. Thayer WATKINS, T. Applet-magic.com-"Office du Niger and the Scheme to irrigate the Sahara Desert"-www.sjsu.edu/faculty/watkins/officeduniger.htm.
6. IMF Data-www.imf.org/external/pubs/ft/scr/2000/cr00126.pdf
7. African Development Bank- Mali-Moyen Bani Program. Appraisal Report and Environmental Impact Assessment Summary. Abidjan.
8. African Development Bank- Mali-Moyen Bani Program. Environmental Impact Assessment Summary. Abidjan.
9. Barbara GRAY-"Framing of Environmental Disputes" in Roy Lewicki, Barbara Gray, and Michael Elliott "Making Sense of Environmental Conflicts. Concepts and Cases." Washington. Island Press. 2003. p 11.
10. Barbara GRAY-"Framing of Environmental Disputes" in Roy Lewicki, Barbara Gray, and Michael Elliott "Making Sense of Environmental Conflicts. Concepts and Cases." Washington. Island Press. 2003. p 20.

Chapter Four

The Conflict

DEFINITIONAL AND THEORETICAL ASPECTS

The linkage between natural resources and conflict is considered to be comparatively recent. In the eighteenth century, Malthus, however, had warned of the possible dangers overpopulation would bring as resources became scarce.[1] These included, but are not limited to, conflicts and war. Alao recognized that conflict does not lend itself to an easy conceptualization.[2] One would be tempted to add that conflict does not lend itself to an easy definition and even less easy categorization. Nevertheless, "conflict" is defined in the Oxford English Dictionary as a disagreement, a dispute, a divergence, a difference, tension, or a controversy. Deng[3] and Nicholson[4] described conflict as a situation of interaction involving two or more parties, in which actions in pursuit of incompatible objectives or interest result in varying degrees of discord. One of the criteria Miall recognized as distinguishing conflict from other situations is that the outcome of the conflict must be considered important to the parties. Miall further contended that because of the great importance of the outcome, political or legal solution must be impossible, and violence would become the last resort.[5] Alao disagreed with this last part, because violence is not always the last resort. He believed instead that often, efforts at "solutions" have not been attempted.[6] Avruch,[7] in combining the definitions of conflict of Lewis Coser[8] and Rubin, Pruitt et al.[9] stated that conflict occurs when two related parties, either individuals, groups, or communities, find themselves divided by perceived incompatible interests or goals in competition for control of scarce resources. The notion of protection and/or control of scarce resources is one of the aspects in Gleick's[10] thinking when he draws parallels to conflicts arising from a situation of scarcity, water scarcity, especially in such water-scarce regions as the Middle East.

In a way, Hirshleifer echoes Coser's concept of seeing conflict as a struggle over claims to scarce resources, whether these are power, status, or natural resources. Hirshleifer brings economic theory into play and sees conflict and predation as being opposed to production and exchange as a way of acquiring resources.[11] He went on to discuss the biological and economic basis of war and conflict. These relate closely to the need for preservation, kinship-preservation and the perception of the level of resources necessary for such preservation, with each party expecting the acquisition of a certain level of resources from the conflict. He made two assumptions about the state of intention of the parties, and these are that both have either benevolent or malevolent intentions towards each other. He also assumes moderate complementarity between the two conflicting parties with each side very optimistic about the return it would get from the conflict. Each party would like to achieve as high a level of the resources in contention as possible, scaled on their respective vertical and horizontal lines. Hirshleifer calls these points unique perception points.[12] They are influenced by, among others, the perception of each party of the amount of already existing resources which each would have to give up in order to achieve higher resources from conflict or war. The relative strength of these resources in achieving the objective is also very critical. The notion of scarcity of food as the ultimate check to population growth discussed by Malthus is in some ways similar to that of Gleick concerning the scarcity of resources and can be linked to Hirshleifer's and Coser's thinking of acquiring scarce resources to the detriment of the other party.

Engel and Korf,[13] as well as Burgess and Burgess,[14] make the distinction between conflict and dispute. All disputes reflect some kind of conflict, but not all conflicts develop into disputes. Nevertheless, a dispute could also be considered as an episode in a conflict. Conflicts tend to be more long lasting and may have several facets. Conflicts involve people's thoughts, emotions, and actions, their feelings and perceptions, and how they frame the conflict with regard to the fundamental issue or issues involved, and also regarding whose fault it is, and how it could be resolved. There are several types of conflict or disputes; Susskind and Cruikshank[15] identify two main types of disputes. There are those which concern constitutional and legal rights and those which relate to resource distributional issues. These latter are linked to the way facilities are sited and include the manner in which land, water and other resources are allocated and utilized.

The second type of dispute, as defined by Susskind and Cruikshank, appears to have some link to Hirshleifer's thinking of acquiring resources, as each party tries to acquire more of the resource in contention or tries to ensure that the amount it has, is not reduced. A link can also be made to Peter

Gleick's notion of conflict over scarce resources. Hirshleifer considers more the economic aspects, whereas Susskind and Cruikshank look more into such issues as perceptions, and emotions. As we had seen earlier, however, these latter feelings though, can influence, as in Hirschleifer thinking, the resources either party would be willing to give up in order to acquire more of the resources in dispute. In terms of definitional categorization, there does not seem to be any hard compartmentalization of these categories. This is because some distributional disputes may have some legal and/or constitutional undertones. This may be an issue when the geographical positioning of a resource-enhancing facility may be linked to the constitutional issues concerning whether the body doing the allocation actually has the right to do so.

This was the case of the Ghana Forestry project, financed by the AfDF and other international financial institutions. The government of Ghana which was promoting the project only had management rights. A conflict arose which concerned the distribution of the revenues from the forest reserves among the central government, the traditional leader and the people who lived in the forest area, with each party claiming a high proportion of the returns under contention. The conflict was resolved after several months in a manner acceptable to all parties, as there was, among the parties, what Hirshleifer would call, both benevolent intentions as well as moderate complementarity. This relatively less protracted resolution was unlike the case with the program under study in Mali. The Ghana case was finalized before the project was even appraised and approved for funding by the AfDF. Ghana is notable, in that all forest, savannah, and woodland reserves are owned by the local communities and traditional authorities, and they are managed by the government in trust for the people.[16] This contrasts with Mali, the country in which the Program under study is located. In Mali, the Government is the legal owner of land and the population enjoys usufruct rights which can be passed on through hereditary process.

In the analysis of the present Program, the central government thus had legal and constitutional powers to allocate resources and to specify where facilities should be sited and where central government funds were to be spent. This latter aspect was being carried out, bearing in mind political considerations, necessary for any elected government. As we had seen in Chapters One and Two, the Moyen Bani Program and the financing by the African Development Fund were approved in 1998 and the loan agreement signed in 1998. However, while the other activities were being implemented in 2001, the main component, which was the construction of the Talo Dam, was well behind schedule because of the controversy which arose. This controversy was the beginning of the conflict. As we had seen earlier, the population of Djenne and the technical preparation and appraisal teams had come to a common understanding of the objective of the Program. Both sides would then have had a common perception of the risk of any reduction in the water flowing downstream from the Talo Dam.

In line with the thinking of Hirshleifer, the unique perception points of the parties concerned would have met at the same point; and the potential settlement region[17] would have been very large. At that time, the issue of the quantity of water reaching the downstream population of Djenne seemed, to have been resolved. The Program was thus approved for funding and implementation of the various activities initiated. One of these was the procurement of a contractor to carry out the major component which was the construction of the dam. The bidding process had been carried out and the bid evaluation results submitted by the Malian government officials for the usual certification by the AfDF. In order to ensure greater clarification and in accordance with established procedures, the AfDF, required the national technical team to re-evaluate the results of the procurement based on the price and technical ability methodology.

THE BEGINNING

Before the team could review and report back to the national selection committee, however, the issue of the adequacy of the water flowing downstream of the Dam resurfaced. This time, it was raised by the Association of Natives of Djenne resident in Bamako (AND). This apparently could be considered an interventional action by the Association. This action modified the common understanding the population of Djenne seemed to have reached with the preparation and appraisal teams during the various consultative and other meetings and sessions they had. It was also a reaction or a response which the Programme elicited that did not seem to have been anticipated, as it was believed, by the central government and the financiers of the Program, that the expected benefits of the Program would be enjoyed by both the population living upstream as well as downstream of the Talo Dam. Olympio Barbanti believes that, in many instances, development interventions tend to underestimate the power of local politics and social realities.[18]

In fact, the Association requested the central government of Mali to refrain from carrying out the dam construction. It felt that the construction will be detrimental to the agricultural activities of the downstream population, whereas the upstream population felt that the dam will help arrest the deteriorating agricultural production which we had seen in Chapters One and Two. This was the beginning of the conflict between the promoters, that is, the government and the upstream population on one side and the downstream population, on the other.

It would be interesting to study the role that the media plays in conflicts and their resolution in rural development activities in Africa. In particular, the role the media played in this conflict. All the details of this conflict and its resolution seem to have been played out in the media. The actions, activities and sentiments of the different parties involved in the conflict and its resolution process were publicized in the media, in the local press as well as in the internet, on the websites of various NGOs.[19] From these, one could garner their sentiments, perceptions and emotions, key aspects which entered into the way they constructed their frames of the conflict. Such publicity, bounty for researchers, may have been carried out in an effort to establish transparency. It could also have been a way to enlist support for the causes of the protagonists in the conflict. Borrowing from Hirshleifer's thinking, this was a way to increase or retain the political and economic resources each of the parties was counting on to ultimately achieve its objective.

Theoretically, and in accordance with the terms of the Framework Law (Loi Cadre) on decentralization discussed in Chapter Two, both the upstream and downstream population had been empowered to elect their own deliberative and executive bodies. These bodies could have discussed possible ways to address the issues and arrive at a solution. But the Loi Cadre had also given the central government oversight over the elected bodies.

As the Program was now appropriated by the central government, the conflict was not just between the upstream population and those in the downstream region, it was also between the central government and the downstream population. To a very large extent, the financiers were cast in the role of "honest brokers." For the funds put by the financiers, at the disposal of the Malian government for the Moyen Bani Program could just as well be made available for another program in Mali. The cost incurred by the financiers, prior to approval, including those for taking the Program through the project cycle and during the conflict, could be considered as "sunk cost." The income expected from lending the funds to Mali, in terms of interest payments would have been the same, had the funds been used for another project or program. From the point of view of the financiers, especially the AfDF, there were a few other programs in Mali, which had been prepared and some appraised which could have been brought forward for approval by the relevant AfDF approving body. Nevertheless, given the nature of its mandate, as is discussed later, the Bank had to help in resolving the issue, even if they could not thus be considered entirely "honest brokers."

Traditional or high context cultures see conflict as a communal concern. In fact it is believed in this case that the Djenne population took ownership of the issue at hand. If it was considered a dispute or a conflict between the upstream and downstream populations, given the high context culture,[20] traditional society existing in Mali, traditional forces of dispute resolution might have been brought into play. For in traditional societies, pathways exist in tribal wisdom for channeling the search for conflict resolutions. Richard Lanek[21] discusses "Mato Oput", which is one of such traditional approaches among the Acholis in northern Uganda. This is an approach which is considered as effective and efficient, especially as it preserves human relationships. There are many other examples of such traditional approaches in many high context cultural societies such as in many African and Asian countries. The papers presented in the All Africa Conference on African Principles of Conflict Resolution and Reconciliation held in November 1999 in Addis Ababa provided several examples of such traditional approaches.

This, however, was not the case in the present conflict. The conflict was seen more as an issue between the central government, promoter of the Program and the downstream population in Djenne, than between the population on either side of proposed Talo Dam. In fact, the upstream population having been convinced and aware of the benefits the Talo Dam would bring to their villages and especially their economic activities like agriculture, fishing and livestock, became impatient with the central government and insisted on resuming the procurement process for the construction of the Talo Dam. The downstream population, on the other hand, insisted on discontinuing all aspects of the project related to the construction of the water regulatory structure. These latter included the Tibi plain development works, and the rehabilitation of the small dam located in Diedala, both of which were not directly in the Talo area. The downstream population feared that these could have negative repercussions on the amount of water reaching downstream. The central government was thus between two conflicting positions. From articles in the local press it could be surmised that tempers and tensions rose to very serious levels. The government had to manoeuvre cautiously between these two positions. This is because conscientious politicians it needed to balance numerous considerations[22].

The central government therefore tried to reconcile two seemingly diametrically opposed positions or frames regarding the Talo Dam. At this point, we can borrow from Hirshleifer and say that there was little or no area of potential settlement, as each party tried to place its expectation at the highest level of their respective imaginary horizontal and vertical lines of resource acquisition. Neither the upstream nor the downstream population seemed to have been very much conscious of the possibility that the resources in contention would be considerably reduced or would no longer exist, if concrete action was not speedily undertaken to preserve them; as the deteriorating climatic situation might seriously affect the resources. In fact, as Avruch[23] would have argued, both parties should have realized that they really have shared interest and goals. The intended structure was expected to increase the resource under contention, which in this case was the total quantity of water available in the River Bani. The non-awareness of the possibility of the resource no longer existing was manifest even though the frames of both parties were economic related as well as being interest and identity related. These three frames were interlinked. The common thread was the adequacy of water which both the upstream and downstream population needed for their respective economic activities.

THE EXTERNALIZATION

It could have reduced tensions had there been direct discussions between the upstream and downstream populations. They were, after all, from very similar, if not the same ethnic background. There were no signs that any previous dispute existed between the two groups of people along the Bani River nor was there any dormant or latent conflict which the construction of the Talo Dam had triggered. Besides, it is well known that traditional and high context cultures follow patterns embedded in the mores and customs of the people.[24] Thus, an amicable solution might have been found to resolve the issue, before it increased in intensity. However, the Association of Natives of Djenne (AND) took the issue up one notch and raised it in the National Assembly in 2000 and requested the central government to stop the construction of the Talo Dam. In addition, in 2001, the AND was able to "triangulize" the conflict further. It got an individual to intervene who, from his website[25] apparently had lived in Mali for some time and had contacts with a nongovernmental organization (NGO) based in the United States of America.

This organization, Cultural Survival, (C.S), took on the issue as a "project", with its own objective, actions, activities, expected outcome, and its own in-house coordinator. The objective became the same as that of the AND. Both wanted the construction of the proposed Talo Dam to be stopped. Cultural Survival felt that the construction was ill-advised, especially with regard to the number of people it was going to displace. The AND believed that the water flowing downstream after the construction would not be adequate for the economic and household activities of the Djenne population. This triangulation,[26] or triangular relationship, brought about a coalition of the population of Djenne, the AND and Cultural Survival. In the context of the conflict at that time, there would appear to have been an inequality of resources, political and otherwise between the two sides. The upstream population seemed to have, as partner, the powerful resources of the central government. This is compared with resources of a population, the Djenne people, in a small part of a vast country of more than one million square kilometers and a national population of around 13 million.

The triangulation could thus be seen as a means of acquiring more resources to contend with the seemingly more powerful resources of the upstream population in the conflict. In a way, this tended to increase the optimism of the downstream population that they would win their case. It thus escalated the conflict when Cultural Survival raised the issue with the AfDB and the embassy of the United States of America (USA) in Mali as well as with the embassy of the USA in Abidjan in Cote d'Ivoire, where the major financier, the AfDB, was based. This would have given the downstream population apparently more political resources, if it could garner the embassy of the USA to its side. Given the sensitivity of the issue and the obviously serious concern raised by the population of Djenne, among others, the central government decided to suspend the construction of the dam and the AfDB decided to suspend the procurement process relating to the dam construction. This suspension, caused by a group with seemingly less political resources compared with those of the upstream population, seemed paradoxical. Factors mentioned earlier contributed to this paradox of power which will be discussed further later on in this chapter.

The suspension of the procurement process and of the construction of the dam appeared to have created further tension with the upstream population and the conflict which was about the volume of water reaching downstream after the construction the Talo Dam changed its nature. Cultural Survival, as part of its activities mentioned previously, commissioned a study of the Moyen Bani Program using the appraisal report as reference. Its study was carried out by Clark University in Worcester, Massachusetts, in the United States of America.[27] The issues raised by the nongovernmental organization included those stated below. These include the loss of downstream agricultural, grazing and fishing land in the target area. The main issue was the volume of water which would be allowed to flow downstream after the construction of the water control structure. The NGO also believed that the potential flooded area would be greater than what the AfDB environmental report indicated and that would lead to more people being displaced than originally envisaged in the preparation and appraisal documents. In a letter to the AfDF published in its website, on its Quarterly Summary, 27.3, Fall, 2003, the NGO also indicated its desire to have the following:

- An environmental impact assessment and socio-economic study focusing on downstream areas from the dam up to the town of Mopti, which is further to the north of Segou;
- An environmental impact assessment focusing on the potential effects of the Talo dam on the greater Niger Inland Delta;

- A revised cost benefit analysis of the potential losses that include both downstream and upstream costs or losses, economic and social, in addition to projected project benefits;
- A comprehensive hydrological study.

The actors in the conflict had now become diverse; they included the AND, the populations upstream of the Talo Dam and those of Djenne who are downstream, as well as the central government of Mali. The upstream and downstream populations are not necessarily homogenous in terms of ethnicity or economic activities. However, they are both regarded as being of high-context cultures, where the notion of the group and human relationships are of the essence. This is contrasted with the other actor, that is, the USA-based non-governmental organization, Cultural Survival, which, Augsburger[28] would have considered as being from a low-context culture. In high context cultures, human relationships are very important and actors believe that there could be situations where both sides come out of the conflict without either losing face and a more win-win situation could materialize. The upstream and downstream population were therefore aware that they have to continue to live together long after the present conflict would have been forgotten. As Cohen would indicate, they would also have been, somehow concerned with the requirements of continuing harmony in the region. Might they have been more willing to explore other modes, mentioned earlier, of searching for alternative solution to resolving the conflict?

Cultural Survival, which came from the low-context culture, tended to have a different perception of how the conflict should be resolved. In their website they insisted that the complementary studies they recommended should be carried out and, most importantly, the construction of the dam should be stopped. In addition, in order to further "triangulize" the conflict, Cultural Survival stated, in its bid to stop the construction of the Talo Dam, that the flooding of the area would adversely affect the third century mosque located in Djenne. For this, it appealed to the United Nations Education Scientific and Cultural Organization (UNESCO) which had designated the Djenne Mosque as a world cultural heritage. By doing so, Cultural Survival was trying to get UNESCO on its side, in a bid to increase its political resources and its clout. In effect, the conflict, with the entry of the NGO, was now viewed by the various parties with different frames which had to be considered in the analysis. Another group of actors or stakeholders in the conflict was the group of financiers, as represented by the major financier the AfDB. This group consisted of legal international entities operating in a low-context culture.

Parties in conflicts often develop significantly different frames about what the conflict is about, what should be done about it, and by whom, it should be done.[29] In the case of the Moyen Bani Program, the point of contention was the quantity of water flowing downstream after the construction of the dam. There was thus the need for the parties to agree on a common basis for describing and measuring the risk of the water flowing down from the Talo Dam being inadequate to satisfy the needs of the economic and household activities of the Djenne population. The Djenne people wanted to ensure that clean water was available for their economic and household activities. How this was done was thus left to the technical teams of both the financiers and the Malian government.

The NGO, on its part, insisted that the quantity envisaged in the design, would not be enough and that the conflict was a purely environmental issue and therefore sought supporters from everywhere. This can be observed from their website in which very negative articles about the Talo Dam were written and appeals were made to the American embassy and the wider internet public.[30] Having succeeded in halting the procurement of the services of the contractor to carry out the works, it would have liked the dam to be taken out of the development equation of the San, Segou, and Bla area. At least two more articles appeared in its websites, one of which requested that all who read the articles should write to the AfDB and the Malian government to stop the Program, indicating an attempt at further triangulation of the conflict.

Why did the NGO add another frame to its initial position? It moved from specifying only technical issues to cultural issues by bringing in UNESCO. Why did it continue further to mobilize the general public? Although its frame could still be considered interest-based, the addition of a cultural flavor to the technical issues made the resolution of the conflict more complex. In this way, the NGO might have believed that by creating a social grievance type movement, it could muster the necessary clout, and increase its political resources as well as the pressure on the Malian government and the AfDB. It expected to succeed in stopping the construction of the Talo Dam. This could be observed from the contents of the articles it wrote on its website. The representative of Cultural Survival at the final meeting, at which the conflict was resolved, indicated that it believed that on its own, it could not have swayed the AfDB and the Malian government to reverse their decision. It felt that as the loans had been approved by both AfDF and OPEC Fund[31], it would not have been easy to stop the implementation.

The public targeted in the web site, however, would have come mainly from the developed countries, given that internet connectivity was not then very common in Mali. There were 0.63 per 10000 persons who were internet subscribers in 1999 and 9.12 persons per 10000 who used the internet in the same year in Mali and 6.7 per 100 subscribers in 2000.[32] Besides, the readership from the developed countries would have been limited to mainly those who were interested in development issues relating to developing countries.

That might have had its limitations in rousing the necessary clout to stop the construction of the dam. This might have been the reason why the NGO got the USAID involved as well as trying to get representatives in Washington, D.C to be involved. Bank staff however, could not recall having received any correspondence from the general public, at that time, following the website appeal.

CONFLICT MANAGEMENT

Before non-African countries joined the AfDB in 1982, the African Development Bank was the creation of countries in Africa with perceptions more akin to high-context culture, even though it was created within the legal, "modern" structure and framework. African political leaders tend to put emphasis on high-context culture type resolution of disputes or conflict. This could be seen in the way the African Union, putting more emphasis on relational issues, tend to have an aversion for decisions which would bring any disruption in the smooth relationship among themselves and their respective countries. Cases in point could be seen in the decisions relating to Uganda during the days of Idi Amin and more recently in those relating to the expulsion from the Union, of Zimbabwe under Mugabe. Most African states had refused or were reluctant to condemn these two leaders openly. Apart from the notion of high-context cultures, there might also be the possibility, for some, that there were also issues which could have been attacked concerning the management of their countries. It is interesting to speculate how the conflict would have evolved under the circumstances of an entirely African ownership of the Bank and the non-existence of the AfDF.

The AfDB of the 1990s however, was quite different from that of the 1970s. In the 1990s, it had shareholding from countries from four continents and was subjected to more low-context type culture pressures. In addition, because their visions and missions are more often couched in economic terms, corporations or international institutions, tend to frame conflict issues in terms of goals, objectives, costs and benefits. Delays to the Program could therefore lead to increased costs and probable non-attainment of objectives or reduction in benefits. It was therefore essential to resolve the conflict as rapidly and as positively as possible. Given the fact that the initial environmental study was not as comprehensive as it should have been, the AfDB, therefore, realized the need for a second look at the environmental issues. The environmental impact assessment of 1995 was complemented with another more comprehensive one in 1997, with more detailed topographical, hydrological, social and economic studies. This made it possible to optimize the dam and to determine precisely the risk of upstream flooding.

The complementary environmental summary indicated there will be no significant negative effect on the downstream area. It appeared then that the concerns of the population of Djenne were not purely environmental.[33] The conclusion drawn was that the issue with the Djenne population was more distributional than environmental with very strong economic undertones. These, relate to the population being able to carry out their economic activities with the volume of water flowing downstream after the construction of the Talo Dam.

As far as the AfDB was concerned, the main point of contention in the conflict thus, reverted to the original frame of distributional issues. Would there be satisfactory quantities of water flowing downstream? Would the overflow be above the level which used to obtain in the past before the droughts? Though this reversion to the issues of adequacy of flow and over flow were "responses" anticipated from the beginning, the potential risks of serious reduction was not precisely gauged and the perception of the risk varied from one party in the conflict to the other. The appropriate measures to address them seemed not to have been adequately incorporated into the design or implementation structure. At that time, the AfDB did not have dedicated conflict resolution section or service, with specific conflict resolution strategies. The local press as well as the website of the NGOs, reported that in a bid to break the deadlock the AfDB and the Malian government undertook information and sensitization missions to the rural areas concerned. The implementation activities on non controversial components had continued, during the conflict relating to the construction of the Talo Dam. Group formation and training were part of these activities and components of the Program and the groups which were established facilitated the sensitization missions and campaign carried out by the AfDB and the Malian governments. These groups included community, farmer and gender based organizations.

The AfDB and the Malian government were under apparent endogenous and non-apparent exogenous pressure to ensure that this protracted and seemingly intractable conflict came to peaceful solution which could be acceptable to all the parties and stakeholders. The exogenous pressure was not apparent, because no one shareholder of the Bank, at that time, exerted any pressure to see the conflict resolved. The Malian government would have been averse to having any armed conflict brewing in the central region as it already had to deal with tensions in the north and east with the Tuaregs. The professor of history and the military general, who succeeded him, must have read military history and conflict, and, would have been aware of the dangers of not peacefully resolving conflicts. In previous years, a lot of negative publicity had spread in the international media about development finance institutions (DFI's) disregarding the concerns of the local population in their interventions. This increased the caution exercised by the external financiers in ensuring that any resolution was acceptable to all parties.

There were also concerns, of generally American- or European-based non-governmental organizations, relating to social and environmental issues concerning the projects these institutions were financing. The NGO's have been leading the charge. The controversy over the environmental aspects of the Massingir Dam in Mozambique, those concerning the gold mine in the region of the Wassa people in Ghana and also those relating to the Bujagali hydro electricity projects are cases in point.[34] Over the years, international NGOs, had been able to acquire a reputation of working in the interest of those unable to speak for themselves. This and other activities tended to legitimize their interventions well beyond the boundaries of their own home bases. It also worked in their favor, as many international development institutions tended to seek legitimacy for their activities, by consulting with or conferring with these international NGO's. Many of the former have set up units or departments within their organizations to deal specifically with NGO's.

The case of the Moyen Bani Program, a distributional conflict relating to the localization of a public good, had now been moved to the international scene. The AfDB had an international reputation to maintain. In 1995, the AfDB had seen its AAA rating in the international money market downgraded to AA+. This meant it would have to borrow at a comparatively much higher rate of interest and more stringent terms than if it had its previous rating. Although the Moyen Bani Program conflict may not have had any direct connection to the rating at that time or to subsequent ratings, the Bank, anxious as it was to get its triple "A" rating restored, was very averse to anything which would throw it into negative light. This is all the more true when we consider that the Bank had not yet fully recovered from the difficult times with lots of negative publicity it had attracted in previous years leading up to the 1995 election of a new president of the Bank; a president, who was elected under a manifesto or program "to make the Bank a bank,"[35] ridding it of all unacceptable practices. Apart from these pressures, the resident executive directors monitored very closely issues relating to the public image of the Bank. It was, in fact, in anticipation of this close monitoring that the senior management of the Bank, ordered the preparation, in 2002, of an information note which gave a chronological report of the conflict and actions taken to ensure that it rapidly came to a satisfactory and peaceful conclusion.[36] For at that time, it had dragged on for well over four years.

The literature[37] indicates that when parties in a conflict have not been able to arrive at a satisfactory solution over several years, the conflict is classified as intractable and maybe that would be the time for a third neutral party, a mediator, to be called to assist. The intractability of the conflict was a result of the modification of frames, which had been influenced by the perceptions of the parties concerned that they would acquire more of the resources under contention if they continued to "fight" for their own position. This would make them remain very high on their respective acquisition lines, leaving little or no area of potential settlement. A neutral and acceptable party was needed to review the different frames and see whether there could be a common understanding or a common ground where all the parties could meet. This would thus bring their perceptions to a level where the potential settlement area could be increased substantially, especially as both sides had much in way of complementarity.

It was recognized that the selection of the mediator was a delicate matter as there are criteria to be seriously considered. Augsburger stated that mediation is not only the ability to define and clarify, to separate and discern, to link and reconcile opposites, but also the capacity to absorb tension, to suffer misunderstanding, to accept rejection, and to bear the pain of others' estrangement.[38] The tension between the upstream and downstream was getting very disturbing and potentially could have led to physical violence. Cohen indicated that in a high-context culture, as that obtaining in the rural areas of Mali, conflict is resolved by mechanisms of communal conciliation, not by resort to formal processes of law. These mechanisms emphasize the importance of "face" and the preservation of "face."[39]

In the present case, the "faces" of both the people in Djenne as well as those in the San, Segou, and Bla region were under threat. Both groups of the major, directly concerned players, had identities specific to their location, defined as "downstream" in the case of the Djenne people and "upstream" in the case of the San, Segou, and Bla people. Another aspect of the frame considered by the Djenne people tended to be diagnostic. They believed that what would jeopardize their receiving adequate quantities of water for their activities was the construction of the dam at Talo. The prognosis was the abandonment of the construction of the proposed dam. The risk aspect, especially their perception of the risk of inadequate water flowing downstream, was therefore, primordial in the minds of the people living in Djenne. Thus, it was believed that, based on their personal histories and experience, the downstream people were unable to accept the analysis of the risk presented by the technical teams of both the African Development Bank and the central government of Mali. In whose analysis, then, could they put their trust? They had no technical team of their own. They found that they could, and were encouraged by both the AND, their own kith and kin, as well as the NGO, to put their trust on the analysis done by the technical team of the NGO.

ATTEMPTS AT RESOLUTION

An impasse had been reached. The conflict and the tension were more or less the same in August 2002 as they were in October 2001. Missions from the Bank and the Malian government continued to organize meetings to inform and sensitize both the upstream and downstream population as to the benefits of the Program. The efforts, at that time, at information and sensitization, apparently turned out not to have had the expected results. Under those circumstances, the role, function, and choice of a mediator was discussed over several months. The crucial criterion is that the mediator chosen should be acceptable to both major parties and that he/she should be neutral and objective. Other adjectives generally used in discussions relating to mediation, include non-coercive, as mediators tend not to have power or sanction to compel parties to follow certain courses, non-binding, non prescriptive, non-threatening, and respected.

The choice fell on a hydraulics engineer who was a former minister of water resources development and also former minister of finance, and apparently well respected in the country. The choice was made in September 2001 for him to assume the role of mediator. Discussions continued about the part he would play in resolving the conflict, especially as the NGO was still insisting on further complementary studies, which, apparently from its website, it hoped would show that the construction of the Talo Dam would be considered as ill advised. Augsburger identifies six types of functions of a mediator. These role types are the following: observer, chairperson, enunciator, prompter, leader and arbiter. However, it is rare for a mediator to play just a single role.[40]

The mediator appointed in the Moyen Bani Program, it could be observed was, in line with the categorization mentioned previously. He combined around three different roles. He was, first and foremost, an arbiter, a facilitator, a go-between the two major parties, which were the upstream and the downstream populations. He was also a prompter, as he contributed suggestions and also helped to clarify issues. He was able to perform the role of chairperson. In the continued search for peaceful resolution, the Malian government, in September 2003, invited the AfDB and the NGO, to a tripartite meeting in Bamako. The NGO was unable to attend due possibly to budgetary or scheduling reasons. This could be considered as tantamount to ill will on the part of the NGO. Its resolve with regard to possible solutions likely to be found in roundtable discussions could be put to question.

In the continued bid to break the impasse relating to the technical issues or differences in opinion between the technical advisers of the NGO and those of the AfDB and the government, the Bank proposed that the NGO designate a reputable expert on irrigation and river flow and the Bank would also appoint an outside specialist consultant to visit Mali and investigate in the field for up to a period of their choice, the potential risks relating to a reduction of flow of water downstream of the Talo Dam. The NGO was unable to make its specialist participate in the mission. It reiterated its concern in its website, as was spelt out earlier in the Clark University report. The Bank specialist carried out the mission. It was confirmed that the protest of the Djenne population was more social and economic than environmental. Following this, the Bank nevertheless reviewed some of the parameters of the previous model in the design, especially as a lot of time had elapsed since the Program was first prepared and appraised. The circumstances in the area had changed.

The information and sensitization campaign continued, and the person being selected to act as mediator participated in the process. This resulted in the establishment of a tentative dialogue between the Ministry of Agriculture and the Association of the Natives of the Djenne residing in Bamako (AND). This, in itself, was a major break-through, as the AND had been the party which had been very reluctant to explore other avenues of resolving the conflict. This paved the way for the government to hold, in February 2003, a widely publicized forum in Djenne on the Moyen Bani Program. Participants at this forum included local elected officials, such representatives of civil society as farmer-, fishermen- and women-based organizations, parliamentary representatives of Djenne, San, and Bla, journalists from the local media, and the mediator designate. It was at this forum that the population of Djenne formalized their request for the construction of a water control structure at the level of Djenne. The major recommendations of what was then called the "Djenne Forum" were the following: acceleration of the finalization of a project to develop the Djenne region; the resumption of works on the Talo Dam. Following this forum, a delegation of representatives of the Djenne population went to Bamako to meet with the prime minister and the president of the Republic to confirm their adhesion to the recommendations of the Djenne Forum.

Nevertheless, the conflict continued unresolved, into November 2003, even though the Djenne Forum had adopted precise recommendations to break the impasse on the management and resolution of the conflict. At that time, it was felt by the AfDB that over and above the technical missions which had been visiting the project area, a more hierarchical clout was needed to resolve the issue both from the point of view of all the parties concerned. Some of the upstream people were not at all happy with their central government for acquiescing to the demands of the AND, which was based in Bamako and not in the rural areas. They must have felt that the members of the AND were enjoying all that the town had to offer. They must have believed that the AND was neither appreciating the hardship caused to their lives in the wake of the drought nor empathizing with the rural upstream population. They were also not happy with the NGO. They were also not pleased with the downstream population either. They seemed to have been even less happy with the government for not continuing with the construction because of the protest of people whom they consider as based in far off land, in the United States of America. There were those from the upstream who felt that this intervention by the NGO could be considered as interference in the affairs of the sovereign government of Mali. Some members of the upstream population raised this aspect, as was reported by the media in the proceedings of the final meeting they had with all the actors in the Program.

Given that Mali was then democratically governed, what the upstream population failed to appreciate was that any objection by an opposition, even a small opposition, to the construction, would affect the perception of the fairness of the government in treating its population. Such a perception by the Djenne population, or by the population of other areas of Mali and more so by the American and Western European governments, which were the major partners supplying funds for development in Mali, would have had a negative effect on the ability of the government to acquire funds in the future for development programs. One must also not forget that the Tuaregs in the north and north-east, were also not very happy and might have felt that their region had been left out in many development programs and any unilateral action by the central government would have been seen by the Tuaregs as a confirmation of the less than equitable way, the government was dealing with the diverse peoples which make up the nation.

The African Development Bank, because of the very nature of its structure, its organization and its major source of finance, would find it difficult to accept that its funds should be associated with a government which rides roughshod over any protest or opposition to the Moyen Bani Program. The executive board of directors, representing the shareholders, kept a short leash on programs and projects financed by the AfDB and the AfDF. The boards were responsible for approving, among others, budget and policy documents. It would have been sorely viewed by the capitals of virtually all the board members for the Malian government to have ignored the discontent of the downstream population.

Serious issues would have been raised, which might have had very negative repercussions on the desire of the Bank to regain its triple "A" rating, or so the senior management of the Bank might have felt. The visit to Mali, by the then vice president responsible for West and Central Africa and his party in November 2003, was very much in line with the wish of both the Bank and the Malian government to resolve this seemingly intractable conflict as peacefully as possible. This should be done by utilizing various compensatory and other strategies of conflict resolution. This conflict had seen the original protagonists joined by others, whose frames or perception of the issue kept evolving and altering, through direct interventional or intentional actions. It was felt therefore by both government and the Bank that they could not afford to continue with the intractability of the conflict.

THE BREAKTHROUGH

It was during this meeting in November 2003, that the Bank, in order to break the impasse, took the decisions summarized below.

- Establishment of a Good Office Committee for Reconciliation and Development, to consolidate the results and achievements of the November 2003 meeting. The committee was to be chaired by the mediator. It was to be comprised of local elected officials, representatives of youths, women and producer associations, as well as residents of Djenne, San, and Segou, and Bla districts. The committee was to work closely with the local administration, local institutions, local traditional and religious authorities;
- Immediate launch (December 2003) of studies to update the environmental and environmental plan, which had been prepared more than six years earlier;
- Conduct of complementary studies to assess the hydrological effects of the dam structure up to the town of Mopti which was an extension of the mathematical model to manage water from the Talo-sill dam reservoir;
- Establishment (in December 2003/January 2004) of the Bani Basin Committee for the management of the Talo dam and follow-up of the studies on the Djenne dam. This was viewed by the central government as an incentive which would make the Djenne population review their objection to the dam and thus allow construction to start. The Bani Basin Committee was to be made up of representatives of all basin users (upstream and downstream), the national and local authorities and the administration;
- Update of the costs of the Moyen Bani Program by February 2004. Costs were finalized in 1997 and therefore needed to be revised;
- Submission to the AfDB in March 2004 of documents for the relaunch of competitive bidding for construction works on the Talo Dam;
- Finalization, by February 2004, of the Terms of Reference for Feasibility Studies for the Djenne dam with a view to present it for consideration to the Board of Directors of the AfDF;

- Formulation, of a program for the conservation and restoration of the Bani Basin with the focal point of the Global Environment Facility (GEF) and the Ministry of Agriculture, Livestock and Fisheries.

The establishment in February 2004 of a Committee of Good Office, chaired by the mediator, gave him a definitely more powerful role than that ordinarily expected of a mediator. The functions of the committee were to inform and to sensitize the riparian population of the River Bani about the development projects on the middle and lower sections of the River. These sections included the dam structures at Talo and Djenne, as well as the riverine plains of Bani from the town called Douna up to Mopti. The committee was also expected to strengthen the communication links between the ethnic groups along the River Bani and the responsible officers of the different development projects along the Bani River. It was also expected to ensure the participation of the riparian population in the management of structures built on the River Bani. This was to be done through their involvement in the Committee for the Management of the Bani River Basin. Finally, their membership of the committee was expected to facilitate the reconciliation among the different actors for the development of the resources of the Bani River Basin. These attributes emphasized the human relational aspects, which, in turn, were expected to enhance effectiveness and also to stress the importance high context culture societies put on them.

A program for the development of Moyen Bani River, especially the construction of a dam at the level of Talo, had been discussed over several years in the past. The mediator, as a former minister of water resources development and also of finance, must have had knowledge of the construction of the dam at Talo and could have actively supported or even promoted its construction. The fact that both the upstream and downstream population accepted him as mediator could be considered a testimony of the respect in which he was held. In addition, he was not external to the culture, as somebody external to the culture might have missed cues and utilized techniques and tactics which could have jeopardized the resolution process. His status as former minister, gave him the clout needed to talk to the then ministers as equal or even as an "elder brother." This status also enabled him to discuss with the officials of the relevant ministries of rural development, local development and others, who would have seen in him as a respected former very senior government official. This attribute contributed to him being able to bring the AND, the strongest opponents of the dam at Talo, to the discussion table, even though for a short period.

During the course of February, March and April 2004, the mediator, convened, chaired, and/or participated in several sessions of the Good Offices

Committee and the Commission for the Management of the Bani River Basin. These meetings as well as the sensitization meetings undertaken by the government contributed significantly to the reduction of tension and a better understanding among the major players in the conflict. The session in April 2004 was chaired by the prime minister who, the local newspaper, l'Essor[41] reported, formally commissioned the members of the Good Office Committee. The presence of this high dignitary of the central government conveyed to the different players the importance the Government attached to resolving the conflict.

With the decision by the AfDB to undertake all the studies demanded by NGO, the technical concerns it had raised were going to be satisfied. As for the downstream population at Djenne, they were able to produce something better than the result they would have obtained without negotiating. They were able to obtain firm commitment from the major financier, that the resources under contention would be shared through the construction of a dam in their own section of the river. It could thus be argued that their best alternative to negotiated agreement would not have yielded them the same result. The Djenne people also were able to obtain the promise of a development program which would contribute to the growth and development of their region. In a way, they traded the acceptance of the Talo Dam for a water control structure of their own. This compensation of a sort is what Weitzman and Weitzman[42] would consider as "bridging." This is defined as creating new options which satisfy their underlying needs for the development of their region, which is the fundamental basis of their interest in receiving adequate flow of water downstream.

Even so, the decision to consider a dam at the level of Djenne was a move not very much appreciated by the NGO, which might have felt that its grip on the conflict process was slipping away. It raised issues of the wisdom of such a structure in its website[43]. This discontent on the part of the NGO is borne even more strongly by the then AND and its president. This latter was still strongly opposed to the construction of the Talo Dam, despite several overtures made to him by the mediator. From articles in the local press at that time, it could be surmised that the then president of AND and one of the then members of Parliament, representing Djenne in the National Assembly, were political opponents. This may have strongly influenced the steadfastness of the perception or frame of the conflict held by the president of the AND.

The NGO, however, could not insist on Djenne not being considered for a water control structure and a development project, as this would really put it in a very bad light, especially with both sides of the proposed Talo Dam having agreed to resolve the conflict and move forward with its construction. Given that its major technical issues against the Program were being actively resolved, the NGO could not therefore refuse to participate in a second meeting, to which the Malian government invited it and the Bank. Apart from the Bank, the government and the NGO, others who participated included the civil society, including journalists in Mali.

It was at this meeting, which was reported in the local media, that the decision-taking representatives of all the major players, as well as those of the Malian government and the major financier, agreed that the conflict had been resolved and that the government and the AfDB could resume the call for bids to implement the construction of the redesigned Talo Dam. In its website, the NGO took note of the efforts of the government since May 2001, at informing, sensitizing and consulting the population with the help of civil society organizations.[44] This consultation was further enhanced when the government and the Bank incorporated the comments and suggestions by participants during the meeting and subsequently those by the Order of Consulting Engineers of Mali, into the terms of reference of the additional studies, which were to be carried out later. Other comments and suggestions incorporated in the final draft of the terms of reference were those from the United States Agency of International Development (USAID).

These additional studies were subsequently carried out by the group of consulting engineers which had been previously retained for the Program. These studies were to be finalized by March 2004 with workshops held for the restoration and validation of the reports. The workshops for validation of the studies were held in May 2004. Participants at these workshops included the International Union for the Conservation of Nature (IUCN), as well as all interested parties, including Cultural Survival. The results of the additional studies showed that the Talo Dam would have negligible or insignificant negative hydrological impact at the level of Djenne and none at the level of Mopti.

All the participants at the meeting, including the USAID, Cultural Survival, agreed that all the outstanding issues have been resolved, and that all the necessary and relevant complementary studies finalized. The May 2004 meeting therefore recommended that the Government should go ahead with the construction of the Talo Dam and also with preparation of the Programme and ultimate construction of a water regulatory structure at the level of Djenne. At the meeting, Cultural Survival, endeavored to justify its intervention as that of an honest and objective adviser on development and agreed to publish, on its website, its satisfaction with the resolution of the conflict. C.S did do this and noted some of the conclusions of the meeting.[45] It was reported that some members of the Djenne population at the meeting requested that the AfDB should take note of the general consensus approving the strategy of the government as it concerned the development of the Bani River Basin. They went on further to request the Bank to accord importance only to true representatives mandated by the people of Djenne. These were construed to mean those residents actually living in Djenne or elected by the people of Djenne.

The epilogue to the management of the conflict was played out in February 2005, when the president of the Republic of Mali, Amadou Toumani Toure, travelled into the interior to officially commission the Coordinating Unit for the Rural Development Program of Djenne and also to lay the corner stone, marking the commencement of works on the Talo Dam. His first stop was at the town of Djenne where traditional, high-context culture ceremonials were very much on the agenda. The importance of relational aspects was very much in evidence. The president of the Republic addressed the audience, composed of traditional chiefs, local, and national elected officials, and members of the government, representatives of the Bank and some members of the diplomatic corps, in French, Bamabara and Peuhl. As we saw earlier, the two latter are the languages of the major ethnic groups in the region. After explaining at length the reason for the Program and the need to construct the Talo and Djenne Dams, he reemphasized that because of the initial opposition to the construction of the Talo Dam, additional studies were carried out. He reiterated that the modifications made to the design of the Talo dam as a result of the studies showed that Djenne and Mopti regions would not be negatively affected.

Here was the president of the Republic, a highly respected and an extremely popular individual, confirming that there was little or no risk of inadequate flow of water to the downstream. The Djenne people believed him. As is customary, and given the initial opposition of the Djenne population to the construction of the Talo Dam, he then, asked them to grant him their authorization to continue his journey to Talo, in order to lay the cornerstone and officially commission the works. This was an act, full of symbolism and traditionalism. Here one has the president of the entire country requesting permission to carry out his duties. Honor, "face" and dignity are very important in a high-context culture.[46] The people of Djenne regained their honor, their dignity and whatever "face" they might have lost in the wrangling and negotiations which got them to the point where they were at that time. The traditional chief of Djenne, speaking on behalf of the whole of Djenne, replied to the president in typical human relational traditional terms saying, "we are behind you", which was understood to mean, "we support and follow you."

The second destination of the presidential party was Talo. The arrival of the party was late because of the various stops by the party to greet the different groups of people who had waited along the roadside to see the president. On arrival in Talo, the president presented his apologies to the waiting spectators for his late arrival and went on to lay the cornerstone, after the usual speeches. The presentation of his apologies for his lateness was another indication of his understanding of the huge importance the people placed on human relational etiquette. This was the final manifestation that the conflict was well and truly resolved.

WHAT WENT WELL AND WHAT DID NOT

The conflict caused a delay of seven years from the time of the approval of the loan by the AfDF in 1998 to the laying of the corner-stone in 2005. During that period, the frames or the perception of the different players underwent a few alterations. The most important of these was the perception of the risk of inadequate flow of water to the downstream population. The downstream population went from accepting the level of risk as presented by the Malian government and the AfDB technical staff as negligible, and raised serious questions after the intervention of the AND. It would appear that the information and sensitization campaign meetings and sessions, undertaken by the government bore fruits. Realizing that they could benefit from the conflict in a more positive way, the Djenne population was able to negotiate their approval of the risk element as enunciated by the technical teams of the Bank and the Malian government. The additional studies which had been agreed upon and carried out contributed to their change of perception. They were able to parlay their acceptance of the Talo Dam against the acceleration of the approval of a development project in their region.

In that regard, though their position and sticking to their position without any compromise had, until then, impeded a speedy resolution of the conflict, they used their acceptance of the construction of a dam at Djenne as a bargaining chip. This cut the ground from under the two other groups more strongly opposed to the continuation of the works on the Talo Dam. These were the AND and the NGO. The Djenne people must have therefore accepted the revised risk analyses of the technical teams after the modifications were made to the design following the additional studies. Otherwise, it would have been contradictory for them to want a dam/ water regulatory structure at Djenne, if they believed that water flowing down to their town was inadequate. The design had been modified to include wider sluice gates to allow more water to flow downstream from the Talo Dam. Several other modifications were incorporated later, following the additional studies and the recommendations of the various meetings held to discuss their results.

Another factor which enhanced the resolution of the conflict was the fact that both the AfDB and the Malian government later became more flexible in their approach to the resolution. For various reasons that had already been discussed, they were both willing to suspend the works on the construction of the Dam until a peaceful resolution accepted by all the major players was reached. It could also be argued that the lapse of time between loan approval and laying of the corner-stone could have been shortened if both the Malian government and the Bank had agreed to carry out the additional studies much earlier. Neither the Malian government nor the AfDB had foreseen or anticipated all the responses the Program would elicit. They were therefore not very well prepared for the conflict to have dragged on for so many years. The first issue was that they did not anticipate that the reference point of risk relating to inadequate water flowing downstream would be challenged through the intervention of the AND and C.S. This was further exacerbated when the NGO, at the start, was unable to sit down and discuss the technical issues, rather, it used its access to the internet, through its web site, to further triangulize the issues.

Why did both the AfDB and the government not agree to undertake the additional studies earlier in the conflict management process? This could be because both parties might have believed that the issue raised by the Djenne population was economic and social, but also that the studies they had commissioned prior to appraisal had produced results which were clear, exact and could not be technically disputed. There could also have been the issue of the involvement of outsiders, that is, an NGO, a non-Africa-based NGO, dictating the course of its proposed or ongoing operations. The costs of additional studies were not negligible and were not provided for in the original budget of the Program. These costs were in addition to the costs of the studies found necessary and carried out in 1997 and 1998 which were also not originally budgeted for. These factors were important considerations earlier on the discussions relating to the reluctance on the part of the AfDB to undertake additional studies for the Program.

The apparent political rivalry, between the then president of the AND, who had invited the USA-based NGO to take the matter beyond the boundaries of Mali and the parliamentary representative, the member of parliament for Djenne was another key factor which enhanced the intractability. One could hypothesize that each party might have been anxious to show the people of Djenne that it could better represent them. This made it more difficult for either of the two to accept any situation which they felt might have compromised the perception of the Djenne people of their individual strength in fighting for their, the Djenne people, interests. The Program thus suffered from the non agreement of these two politicians. The notion of a group of residents of a village or a town in the interior setting up an association in the capital city is in itself a very laudable idea. The capital is the seat of government and decision making. Having a group in the capital, working for the interest of their towns mates in the interior of the country would serve as a lobbying group with the government ministers and other decision makers. The group must be in synchronization with those of their town's mates on whose behalf they are supposed to lobbying. However, as was seen in the preceding analysis, there came a time when the AND and the population in Djenne were not singing from the same page let alone the same line. This was seen at the time when the Djenne population had successfully negotiated a resolution of the conflict and a development project for their region and the AND, or more specifically, its president at that time, was still opposed to the construction of the Talo Dam.

The differences in frame or perception of the risk involved could also be considered an impediment to the speedy resolution of the conflict. The perception of the level of risk that was most important, was that of the Djenne population; and this kept changing, mainly through intentional interventions of the AND and the NGO. This retarded the finding of an acceptable solution. Had there been many more information and sensitization activities prior to the preparation and appraisal of the Program, there might have been a better understanding by the Djenne population at appraisal. To a large extent, this situation has improved with the current production, by most developing countries, of Poverty Reduction Strategy Papers (PRSP). The PRSP and the process leading to its preparation and subsequent approval by the relevant authority in the countries, would provide a large forum where all the various groups at the different locations would be informed of socio-economic development activities being proposed for theirs and the surrounding areas. The diverse views would then be aired, the issues discussed and a consensus agreed upon. Information and sensitization required concerning any development program or any specific project could then start very early in the project cycle, before the program design documents are finalized.

EXTERNAL ASSISTANCE OR EXTERNAL INTERFERENCE?

Was the externalization of the conflict a positive or negative factor? Did it aggravate the conflict and made it harder to find a solution? Was there any positive value to this externalization? Did the NGO consciously or unconsciously manipulate the AND and from there, the Djenne population? Did the frame adopted by the America-based, low context culture NGO affect its perception and by extension, the conflict management? Finally, could its intervention be considered a worthwhile assistance, a hindrance to development or interference in the affairs of a sovereign state?

The externalization of the conflict could be considered as having had the effect of protracting the conflict. This is because it could be argued that the

Djenne population would have started to negotiate with their central government much earlier than they did. The traditional paths of dispute resolution through elders and traditional chiefs could have been brought into play much earlier. However, the externalization had the effect of making the case of the Djenne population much better known and this contributed to their obtaining a deal which they might not have had, had the external NGO not entered into the equation. As regards the NGO, its intervention, judging from their website, "taking up the case of the Djenne people", was "project" and part of their program of activities. These had objectives and expected outcomes. The original objective, again, from their website, was to arrest the construction of the Talo Dam. In order to strengthen their hand, they commissioned the study by Clark University which brought "technical issues" into play. Clark University could thus be considered their "technical lawyers" and passive advocates.

Such technical issues, assuming that the University team spent as much time in the field as did the previous teams of consulting firms, government experts, and experts from the financiers had the effect of casting doubt on the parameters and assumptions of the previous studies. Publicizing it on its website was another way to get further attention. A further instrument used by the NGO was to invite USAID to be aware of this and thus further making it very difficult for the promoters and financiers to ignore its position. USAID/REDSO later visited the dam site with a team from the promoters and sponsors, and concluded that the issue was economic and social and not environmental as was later shown.

NGOs from developed countries have shown a great propensity to intervene in projects and programs undertaken in lands far away from their own national territories. A few instances have been submitted earlier. In fact, especially in the case of NGOs based in the United States of America, they have a tendency of trying to boost their clout by requesting the parliamentary representative or senator to intervene with the Administration in Washington, D.C. This was expected to produce a chain reaction through which the federal Administration would intervene in the country concerned through the local USAID office or its representative in the Board of Directors, if it is an institution in which it is represented or through the ambassador in the country. This would provide strong enough political and/or economic clout to trigger a change in the action of the country as regards the issue at hand.

This is in line with the thinking of Hirshleifer, whereby parties in conflict endeavor to acquire resources, political and/or economic, which would help them to obtain more of the resource under contention. Such acquisition would contribute to them attaining their goal, whether it is getting more resources or stopping the other party from getting any at all. A case in point occurred in

2004 and had to deal with the parastatal organization corporation, Office du Niger in Mali. A missionary who had lived in Mali over twenty years learnt that Office du Niger had plans in a particular project to displace farmers who had cultivated the land for decades. The displaced farmers were expected to receive funds from the USA financed Millennium Challenge Fund (MCF). With the apparent assistance of the missionary, the villagers wrote to the Malian government so that they would not lose their homes. The missionary provided the triangulizing frame. She wrote to her supporters in Oklahoma and they wrote to their state senator who apparently got other NGOs in Washington, D.C involved and they built up the protest, and publicized it. MCF investigated and found some untoward practices and claims, and the action of Office du Niger was stopped.[47]

This was much the same strategy that Cultural Survival had used earlier in 2000. Several other NGOs have used similar strategies in the past as was seen in the case of the Bujagali hydroelectric project in Uganda. The web campaign carried out recently by an NGO to stop the construction of the Gibe III dam project in Ethiopia is another example of this strategy. The citing of these examples does not question the merits or demerits of the argument on either side of the issues involved. It is in order to demonstrate the role NGO's are playing in the whole process of harnessing the resources of a developing country for the improvement in the wellbeing of the nationals.

In the case of the Moyen Bani Program, the NGO, at the final meeting held in Mali, explained to the people of the areas concerned that it acted "in its capacity as adviser for a better development." Was there a specific agreement between the AND and the NGO for it to act as its adviser? There did not seem to have been any such agreement or contract; and generally, NGOs tend not to wait for agreements or invitation to get involved in protests around the world. It might be said, though, that in the case of the Moyen Bani Program, Cultural Survival did get an "invite" of a sort from the then AND president in Bamako. A tendency has been observed whereby international NGOs endeavor to obtain "invites" from local NGOs with similar missions, in order to "legitimize" their interventions. In the case, mentioned previously, of the gold mining Project in Ghana, the local NGOs were also mobilized and had worked with the international NGOs. Nevertheless, judging from the action and activities of Cultural Survival, one would want to believe that it went beyond the mandate of any "adviser." An "adviser", granted, would undertake specific studies as necessary, for he/she to be able to "advise." This would be in order to ensure the right advice is given. The study commissioned with Clark University could be considered in this light.

One wonders however, whether an adviser has the right to publicize a conflict it is advising on, in its website and to ask the general public to protest and write letters, and emails to the institution financing the aspect of the development under contention as well as to the Government promoting it. That is more the role NGOs have devolved upon themselves, over the years, as what is known in the development context as the "third sector." The first two sectors are the state/government and the private corporations. In that respect, NGOs tend to claim neutrality and insist on their "not-for-profit" status, which tends to help them in their discussions with the two other parties. These two aspects are claimed by them to confer objectivity in any protest in which they participate. Note must be taken of the fact that the term "NGO" hides a vast gamut of different and similar organizations operating in different geographic, referential, interest and spatial domains. Some of these are very well structured and organized whereas others are not so well organized or even structured at all. Some are one subject interest groups, while others have multiple interests. They exist in many countries and all continents. The body of literature which has developed over the years, while accepting the very useful work that has been and is being done by NGOs, question some aspects of their actions and activities.

One area which has come under scrutiny is that of their neutrality, especially that part which is enhanced by the not-for-profit status which many of them tend to claim. In an online article in "Global Issues," Anup Shah[48] effectively raises questions about these aspects. He states that NGOs are meant to be politically independent, but in reality, it is a difficult task, because they must receive funding of their activities from government, other institutions, business, and/or private sources. It is to be noted also the make-up of their boards of directors or boards of governors could also influence their actions or non-actions. It could be argued that all of these can have direct or indirect political and/or economic/financial weight on decisions and actions of the NGOs. This tends to cast shadows of doubt on the aspect of neutrality. He went on to discuss the image NGOs have of themselves as neutral actors, brokering relations among the business, state, and civil society.

It is an open question where these bodies, especially the international NGOs, receive the authority to act as neutral parties. They may argue, though, that, before any such body operates within a geographic entity it has to be registered, with its aims, mission, and general objectives declared. They may take this registration as an authority to operate, as they may be made accountable not only to their board of directors but also to the registering authority in the state, which may or may not have its own monitoring mechanisms. Where do the international NGOs which are not registered in a state get their authority to intervene in the affairs of the state, as did Cultural Survival? Such a body is accountable to its own board located away from the states they operate or intervene in, and also to its financial backers. It could be argued that in the present "global village," environmental concerns do not have boundaries as environmental incidents in one area could affect another area in a different part of the globe. This would therefore, some people may contend, justify NGOs based in one part of the world to intervene in another. While this may true in certain cases, it would be far-fetched to draw a conclusion of similarity, in the case of the Moyen Bani Program,

As has been seen earlier, the action of Cultural Survival in publicizing the protest may therefore, have been considered in its own eyes, an act of empowering the local people, in this respect, the people of Djenne, and help making their voices heard well beyond the shores of their own homeland. Whether one agrees or disagrees with its intervention in the Moyen Bani Program, one cannot but grant that it was effective in doing that. The externalization of the conflict could be considered as having had the effect of protracting the conflict. It could be argued that the Djenne population would have started to negotiate with the Malian government much earlier than they did.

Did the fact that the voices of the Djenne population were heard beyond the shores Djenne and Mali help the Djenne population in advancing its socio-economic development agenda? From the preceding analysis, one may be given to think that it did; as they were able, not only to suspend, for a long period of time, the construction of the Talo Dam, but also to obtain a firm promise from the government and the major financier, that they would have their own development project and their own water regulatory structure. This could be considered, by Fischer and Ury,[49] as their best alternative not necessarily to negotiation, but to stopping the Talo Dam construction. It can also be seen from the analysis, that the traditional pathways of conflict resolution may have been invoked much earlier on, where the various frames or perceptions of the different players could have been heard and the issues resolved and their own needs catered for.

Another issue, often raised with regards to NGOs operating away from their home base, is that concerning the frame or perception of the issues at hand. In the case of the Moyen Bani Program, the perception of Cultural Survival of conflicts in rural areas of the developing countries could be called to question. Many of these international NGOs operating in Africa, for example, have their headquarters in non-African territories. The cultural perceptions of the organization tend to be different from those of the countries in which they operate and intervene, even though high-context cultures may be tending towards low-context culture behavior through the process of modernization. Their perceptions tend to be that of low-context cultures whereas the predominant frame of thinking in many developing countries tends to be more human relational and high-context. If these international NGOs employ staff members from developing countries who grew up and were trained in high-context cultures, to work on their out-of-home-base operations in high context settings, would these staffers be considered as having high-context culture thinking or would they still be considered as having low-context culture mind set? Would the organizational or corporate low-context culture perceptions instead predominate in their thought processes and actions?

The question could therefore safely be asked whether Cultural Survival deeply understood the complexities of the relationships in the Moyen Bani conflict. There is nothing in any written statement or declaration which could be cited to indicate that the NGO did not understand the complexities of the relationship in the conflict. However, in traditional societies which tend to be high context culture societies, there are subtleties which may escape the uninitiated. In such a society, as is the Malian society, an invitation from a minister or the prime minister, who is regarded as the "Bwana kuba" in East African Swahili or the "Ogah" in Yoruba, (in other words, the "big man or boss,") had to be honored. This had to be done, even if one did not agree with the "big man" or one would not agree with what he was going to say; unless, of course the invitee believes that there could be a life threatening situation. The minister of agriculture had invited the NGO to a tripartite meeting with the AfDB, at which the parties from Djenne and the Bla, Segou, and San area, were going to be present. The NGO was unable to honor the invitation, or even send a low level representative, which, in a way, would have marked its discontent with the process. This could be considered an act which is tantamount to not being aware of certain protocol of high-context culture societies. Furthermore, the seeming unwillingness and/or inability of the NGO to discuss or participate in any technical mission with the Malian government and the AfDB, until its demands were met, were another manifestation of someone from a low-context culture. In the latter culture, there is a tendency of parties to feel that it is an "all or nothing" situation or "either I win and you lose or vice versa" situation.[50]

To this end, the association of the NGO with the Association of Natives of Djenne resident in Bamako, was mutually beneficial. Through this relationship, the AND was able to get wider publicity for its cause which was based on the opposition to the construction of the Talo Dam. As it were, the NGO "obtained an invitation" to get involved in a conflict which it saw as part of its mission. This "invitation" might have been seen by the NGO as giving it "legitimacy" in its intervention. With that said, international NGOs do not seem to require invitations, for them to consider intervening in any issue which they consider as part of their world mission. Nevertheless, the "invitation" from the AND could be considered a boost to its intervention in the conflict. With regard to the question of manipulation, no strong evidence or argument that Cultural Survival knowingly manipulated the AND, and, by extension, the Djenne people, could be found. It could be argued, though, that its earlier inability to discuss or participate in any technical mission, quite apart from making the conflict more intractable, could also be considered a possible manipulation, because this strengthened the earlier resolve of the Djenne people and the AND not give in to the position of the government and the people of Segou, Bla, and San.

From the above discussion and analysis, it could be observed that the Republic of Mali, by virtue of it being a developing country without strong foreign currency reserve, had to depend and still depends on external assistance to move its development agenda forward. The high proportion of external aid to Mali was noted in Chapter Two; this was 16% of GNP and US $57.9 billion in 2000 according to World Bank.[51] Net domestic financing for the average of 2002–2005 was a negative of CFAF 26.8 billion, according to AfDB and OECD.

External assistance comes, as has been seen earlier, with its own conditions. Most of the international development finance institutions had, and some still have, conditions which have to be fulfilled. Some of these are precedent, which means that they have to be fulfilled before any disbursement could be made. Others have to be fulfilled during the course of the implementation of the project or programme. As seen in Chapter Three, the Moyen Bani Program had several conditions of both types. In general, these conditions could, in any one project, vary from specific ad hoc conditions, directly concerned with project management (e.g. the appointment of a Program director and key staff), to such others, as the ones which relate to the establishment of a development committee or the study on tariffs and rates. These latter conditions and the ones related to the study of costs of maintenance of hydraulic structures and ensuring that the recommended tariffs were applied were more far reaching and policy oriented. The condition relating to the government providing funds for ensuring extension services to farmers, farmers and village associations related more to instructions concerning budgetary allocations, even though it was mentioned "in accordance with the financing plan." These and other conditions were intended to contribute to ensuring smooth implementation.

In some ways, they covered for those responses which the program would have elicited, and which had to be taken on board, but were not allowed to delay the implementation of the Program. Otherwise, it would be fair to assume that the promoters and financiers should have ensured that these conditions were met before the program was even approved. Whatever the position taken on these conditions, they could be viewed as interference in the normal business of the government, which would not have been necessary, had the government not solicited funds from outside its borders.

This, one could contend, is "necessary interference", as the development activities which came with it, could not have been obtained otherwise. Was there any positive result from the intervention of Cultural Survival in the conflict? Its intervention did not, in any way, immediately resolve the conflict or allow the Program to move forward. Nevertheless, its intervention brought greater attention to the issue of the Talo Dam and gave "improved or louder" voice to the position of the Djenne population. By commissioning a study of the Program, Cultural Survival might be considered as having provided a "second opinion" with regard to the different parameters and risks involved with the development of the dam. Its intervention instigated a second look at the sluice gates and encouraged the technical specifications to be modified, which was to lead to even more water flowing down stream. Its insistence on complementary studies and with these showing negligible impact on river flow up to Mopti in the North, helped to reassure the Djenne people that their economic activities would benefit from the construction of the Talo Dam.

These studies also eliminated any other possible issues or conflict which might have been raised later by the population further downstream at Mopti. These are positive aspects however, which, some would argue, do not compensate for its contribution towards the intractability and lengthening of the period of conflict resolution. It could thus be argued that on a scale of positive on one side and negative on the other, external assistance in general, with emphasis on "in general", irrespective of which side of the political or economic fence one is situated, tend to be very slightly towards the positive, especially in many developing countries. Those developing countries, with weak capital resources, poor external reserves, weak organizational systems, weak national oversight or audit system, and weak international political clout, tend to be more vulnerable to interventions from international NGOs. Some emerging countries, with strong political and/or economic clout are not very much influenced by protests or "interventions" by NGOs, international or local. The Three Gorges Dam over the Yangtze River in China is a case in point. Construction, which started in 1994, went ahead, in spite of international protests and the World Bank withdrawing support for the project.

There are situations and circumstances, though, where external assistance could be considered as purely external interference. These often relate to situations where international NGOs and other bodies are endeavoring to impose their own economic, political, social or cultural ideologies or their own self-interest-based development agenda on a country. Depending on the organization or body, its financial and/or political backing, such imposition can be overt or covert. Could the NGO be considered as having made such an imposition? Given the very specific and technical nature of its demands, no such ideological imposition is evident. However, the fact that it stated that it acted as adviser to AND, and, in addition, by publicizing its views and its discontent with the Talo Dam, it was overtly putting forward the ideology of empowerment of the Djenne people as a social concept. Among others, the merits and demerits of this action depend on whether there exist in the society, avenues and resources for civil society organizations to be empowered, what they should be empowered for or even the necessity of their being empowered. This, however, is not the subject of this book.

NOTES

1. Thomas MALTHUS, "An Essay on the Principle of Population", Library of Economics and Liberty (http://www.econlib.org). Please link to the original URL, http://www.econlib.org/library/Malthus/malPlong.html. Book I.II.1–9.

2. Abiodun ALAO, "Natural Resources and Conflict in Africa. The Tragedy of Endowment." Rochester: University of Rochester Press. 2007. p 18.

3. Francis DENG, "Anatomy of Conflict in Africa" in "Between Development and Destruction: An Enquiry in the Causes of Conflict in Post Colonial State." Ed. Luc Van de Goor, Kumar Rupesinghe, and Paul Sciarone. The Netherlands Ministry of Foreign Affairs (DGIS) in association with The Netherlands Institute of International Relations, CLINGENDAEL. The Hague. 1996. p 220.

4. Michael NICHOLSON, "Conflict Analysis." London: English University Press, 1970. and Barnes & Noble Inc. 1971. Page 2.

5. Hugh MIALL, "The Peace-Makers: Peaceful Settlements of Disputes since 1945." London: MacMillan. 1992.

6. Abiodun ALAO, "Natural Resources and Conflict in Africa. The Tragedy of Endowment." Rochester: University of Rochester Press. 2007. p 19.

7. Kevin AVRUCH, "Culture and Conflict Resolution" Washington, D.C. United States Institute of Peace. 1998. p 24.

8. Lewis COSER, "Functions of Social Conflict: An Examination of the Concept of Social Conflict and Its Use in Empirical Sociological Research." New York: Free Press. 1956. p 8.

9. J. RUBIN, D. PRUIT, and S. KIM, "Social Conflict: Escalation, Stalemate, and Settlement." Second edition. New York: McGraw-Hill 1994. p 5.

10. Peter GLEICK, "Water and Conflict: Freshwater Resources and International Security" in 'International Security', 18 (1). Summer 1993. Also International Water Resources, Chapter Two, sections 2.2 and 2.3.1. CA and CC Press. AB Publishing House. Sweden.

11. Jack HIRSHLEIFER, "The Dark Side of the Force. Economic Foundations of Conflict Theory." Cambridge: Cambridge University Press. 2001. p 1.

12. Jack HIRSHLEIFER, "The Dark Side of the Force. Economic Foundations of Conflict Theory." Cambridge: Cambridge University Press. 2001. p 27.

13. Antonia ENGEL and Benedikt KORF, "Negotiation and Mediation Techniques for Natural Resources Management." Rome: Food and Agricultural Organization of the United Nations. 2005. Page 20.

14. Guy BURGESS and Heidi BURGESS, "Environmental Mediation: Beyond the Limits Applying Dispute Resolution Principles to Intractable Environmental Conflicts" Conflict Research Consortium. Working Paper 94–50 February 1994. p 2.

15. Lawrence SUSSKIND and Jeffrey CRUIKSHANK, "Breaking the Impasse. Consensual Approaches to Resolving Public Disputes." New York: Basic Books, Inc. 1987. p 17.

16. African Development Bank, Ghana Forestry Project. Abidjan.

17. Jack HIRSHLEIFER, "The Dark Side of the Force. Economic Foundations of Conflict Theory." Cambridge: Cambridge University Press. 2001. pp 27, 29.

18. Olympio BARBANTI, jr, "Development and Conflict Theory." "Beyond Intractability." August 2004. p 2. www.beyondintractibilty.org/essay/development. Also Brehima TOURE, "Mali barrage de la discorde" in Syfia-Mali : www.syfiainfoindex.php.5?view&action&idArticle=502.

19. "Mali- Barrage du discorde" in www.syfia.info. Also "Projet Moyen Bani: le seuil de Talo sort de la controverse" www.essor.ml, issues 15193, 15916. Also "Developpement du bassin du Bani: feu vert pour PDRI/Djenne" in www.malikounda.com. Also "Talo Dam" http://Djenne-patrimoine.fr/racine/dp19htm. and djenneinitiative.org. Also "The Djenne Project in Mali" *Cultural Survival Quarterly* issues 25(2), 28 (1), 28(3) www.culturalsurvival.org.

20. David W. AUGSBURGER, "Conflict Mediation Across Cultures. Pathways and Patterns." Louisville. London. Westminster John Knox Press. 1992. pp 28–35.

21. Richard LANEK. "Traditional Approaches among the Acholis in Northern Uganda." Paper presented at the All Africa Conference on African Principles of Conflict Resolution and Reconciliation. Addis Ababa, Ethiopia. November 1999.

22. Lawrence SUSSKIND and Jeffrey CRUIKSHANK, "Breaking the Impasse. Consensual Approaches to Resolving Public Disputes." New York: Basic Books, Inc. 1987. p 9.

23. Kevin AVRUCH, "Culture and Conflict Resolution." United States Institute of Peace. 1998. p 25.

24. David W. AUGSBURGER, "Conflict Mediation Across Cultures. Pathways and Patterns." Louisville. London. Westminster John Knox Press. 1992. Pages 6 and 8.

25. The Djenne Initiative Inc. At: www.djenneinitiative.org.

26. David W. AUGSBURGER, "Conflict Mediation Across Cultures. Pathways and Patterns." Louisville. London. Westminster John Knox Press. 1992. pp 148, 155.

27. CLARK University, Report on the Talo Dam in Mali. See www.clarku.edu and also www.culturalsurvival.org.

28. David W. AUGSBURGER, "Conflict Mediation Across Cultures. Pathways and Patterns." Louisville. London. Westminster John Knox Press. 1992. p 8.

29. Roy LEWICKI and Barbara GRAY, "Introduction" in Roy LEWICKI, Barbara GRAY and Michael ELLIOTT, Eds. "Making Sense of Intractable Environmental Conflicts. Concepts and Cases." Washington. Island Press. 2003. p 13.

30. Deidre d'ENTREMONT, "The Djenne Project, Mali." Jean Louis Bourgeois, Coordinator. *Cultural Survival Quarterly*. Issue #25.2. July 31, 2001. p 2. Also MANSA Newsletter, no. 45, Winter 2000-2001.

31. Mali. Moyen Bani Program. Project Completion Report at: http://www.afdb.org/fileadmin/uploads/afdb/Documents/Project-and-Operations/Mali. Middle Bani Plains Development Programme _FR.pdf.

32. United Nations Economic Commission for Africa. See www.uneca.org/aisi/nici/country_profiles/mali/malinter.htm. and http://ddp-ext.worldbnk.org/ext/ddpreports/ViewSharedReport?R.

33. African Development Bank. "Information Note on Talo Dam in Mali." Abidjan.

34. Eighth World Wilderness Congress. Resolution #16. September 30—October 6, 2005. Anchorage, Alaska. *Also* Jim CASON "Africa: Controversy Continues to Dog Major World Bank Project" In CORPWATCH. April 25, 2002. At: www.corpwatch.org/article.php?id=2410. Also Friends of the Earth at: www.foe.org/international-work/world-bank-background.

35. Andrea DAVIS, "On the Rocks: The African Development Bank Struggles to stay Afloat." July 1, 1996. Multinational Monitor. www.allbusiness.com/speciality-business/581033-1.html.

36. African Development Bank. "Information Note on Talo Dam in Mali." Abidjan.

37. Lawrence SUSSKIND and Jeffrey CRUIKSHANK, "Breaking the Impasse. Consensual Approaches to Resolving Public Disputes." New York: Basic Books, Inc. 1987. pp 28–35. Also David W. AUGSBURGER, "Conflict Mediation Across Cultures. Pathways and Patterns." Louisville. London. Westminster John Knox Press. 1992. p 191.

38. Lawrence SUSSKIND and Jeffrey CRUIKSHANK, "Breaking the Impasse. Consensual Approaches to Resolving Public Disputes." New York: Basic Books, Inc. 1987. Page 142. Also David W. AUGSBURGER, "Conflict Mediation Across Cultures. Pathways and Patterns." Louisville. London. Westminster John Knox Press. 1992. p 191.

39. Raymond COHEN "International Communication in an Interdependent World. Negotiating Across Cultures." Revised edition. Washington, D.C. 1997. United States Institute of Peace Press. p 32.

40. David W. AUGSBURGER, "Conflict Mediation Across Cultures. Pathways and Patterns." Louisville. London. Westminster John Knox Press. 1992. pp 86–96, p 194.

41. Report on Mali Talo Dam at www.essor.ml.

42. Eben A. WEITZMAN and Patricia Flynn WEITZMAN, "Problem Solving and Decision Making in Conflict Resolution" In "The Handbook of Conflict Resolution: Theory and Practice." San Francisco: Jossey-Bass Publishers. 2000. pp 185–209.

43. Larry CHILDS, "Talo Dam Construction Delay Holds: African Development Bank and Malian Government Implement Cultural Survival Recommendations." *Cultural Survival Quarterly*. March 15, 2004. 28(1). p 2.

44. Justine PETRILLO, "Cultural Survival Endorses Revised Plan for Talo Dam Construction." *Cultural Survival Quarterly*. September 15, 2004. 28(3). p 1.

45. Justine PETRILLO, "Cultural Survival Endorses Revised Plan for Talo Dam Construction." *Cultural Survival Quarterly*. September 15, 2004. 28(3). p 1.

46. Raymond COHEN "International Communication in an Interdependent World. Negotiating Across Cultures." Revised edition. Washington, D.C. United States Institute of Peace Press. 1997. p 32. Also David W. AUGSBURGER, "Conflict Mediation Across Cultures. Pathways and Patterns." Louisville. London. Westminster John Knox Press. 1992. pp 86–96.

47. Christian Reformed Church, Office du Niger. OSJ. www.crcna.org/pages/officeduniger.cfm.

48. Anup SHAH, "Non-Governmental Organizations on Development Issues." In Global Issues. June 01, 2005. www.globalissues.org/article/25/non-governmental-organization.

49. Roger FISHER, William URY, and Bruce PATTON, "Getting to Yes. Negotiating Agreement without Giving In." Second edition. New York: Penguin Books. 1991. p 99.

50. David W. AUGSBURGER, "Conflict Mediation Across Cultures. Pathways and Patterns." Louisville. London. Westminster John Knox Press. 1992. p 50.

51. World Bank Group. "Mali at a Glance." September 24-2008. At www.worldbank.org.

Chapter Five

The Conflict and Post Conflict Period

IMPLEMENTATION, MONITORING AND RESULTS

The conflict was considered finally resolved in April 2005. The post conflict period from 2005 to 2007, was therefore utilized to rapidly implement the various components of the Program. Some of these components had been delayed since 2000. The most important of these was the construction of the Talo Dam. The bidding process was resumed, a contractor was selected and the construction of the dam started in earnest. Table 5.1 gives details of the implementation of some of the key activities under the Program.

The data in Table 5.1, confirm that some non-controversial activities were being carried out, as previously indicated. In addition, some of the activities took longer than scheduled in the ex ante implementation. This is the case of the execution of the wells which were scheduled to be completed in not more than five months, but were completed in twelve months. None of these however, were due to the conflict with the construction of the Talo Dam. Other activities, such as development of the land and the road development works were in the critical path of the construction of, and were closely linked to, the dam. They were thus affected by the conflict. They therefore had to be implemented in tandem with the dam. Others, such as the development of small irrigated perimeters were delayed, not because of the conflict, but as a result of the contractor not respecting the prescribed monitoring benchmarks and indicators.

With regard to the construction of the dam, the development of the plains and the road network, they were implemented in accordance with the schedules, which were revised after the conflict was considered resolved. The construction on the three civil works mentioned earlier was finalized within

Table 5.1. Implementation of Major Activities

Type of Activity	Date Contract Notification	Start Date Implementation	Date of Completion	Duration in Months
Construction of Offices	12/11/1999	30/11/1999	01/03/2000	4
Construction of Large wells	01/07/2003	09/04/2003	01/04/04	12
Development of small perimeters- lot II	18/03/2003	05/01/2004	15/05/2007	40
Development of small perimeters- lot I	N/A	28/04/2003	22/07/2004	15
Construction of Dam- lot I	28/02/2005	15/04/2005	12/01/2007	21
Development of Plains – lot II	28/02/2005	15/04/2005	16/01/2007	21
Road Construction- lot III	04/05/2005	15/05/2005	08/08/2006	21
Agricultural Development Works	10/01/2007	17/03/2007	31/05/2007	02
Construction of Fencing-Health Centers	18/04/2003	28/04/2003	22/07/2004	15
Construction of Fencing – Health Centers-Koro	18/04/2003	28/04/2003	08/07/2004	15
Construction of four large wells	04/09/2001	28/09/2001	20/01/2002	04
Construction of nine wells	18/10/2005	02/11/2005	05/04/2006	05

Source: Adapted from the Project Completion Report Moyen Bani Program. First Phase—African Development Bank

twenty months. This was much earlier than the initial implementation programs which had been scheduled to take between forty and forty-two months as shown in Table 5.2. This actual construction implementation period was influenced by the contractor putting a large number of workers on the sites. In addition, it could also be argued that the initial implementation programs were ex ante estimates made by the preparation and appraisal teams based on experiences of similar past projects, discussions with potential contractors in the field and before any actual bidding was done. The revised implementation period after the conflict, was the contractors' estimates based on their own experiences and the final period is the actual ex post figures. It should be

Table 5.2. Summary of Initial Implementation Programme of Key Activities

Type of Activity	Start Date of Completion	Date of Completion	Duration in Months
Recruitment of Consultants	06/98	12/98	6
Civil Works on Dam	10/98	06/02	44
Land Development Works on Perimeters	01/99	06/02	41
Crop cultivation	07/02/	N/A	N/A

Source: Adapted from the Project Completion Report Moyen Bani Program. First Phase—African Development Bank

noted also that the modifications made to the design of the dam had no negative influence on the construction period. These modifications which were the result of suggestions, comments and studies should have theoretically tended to lengthen the implementation period of the dam. However this was not the case and the reverse took place. The performance of the contractors who carried out the major civil works was considered by the program management team as very satisfactory.[1] This relatively early finalization of the major construction work helped to reduce the negative impact on the final cost/benefit analysis, of the time taken to successfully resolve the conflict. Crop cultivation started earlier than if the initially programed construction period of forty-four months was actually used up.

It can be observed in Table 5.1 that the startup period for the major contractors, for the dam, the road construction, and the land development, varied in general from eleven days for the road network development, to two months for the dam construction to nine months for the construction of large wells. Nine months preparation start-up period appears substantial for the well construction and the development of small irrigated perimeters, as compared with that of the dam construction, a much larger civil work, which took two months. It is very important to factor the startup period for implementation of Program activities into the implementation schedule.

The post conflict period was also used to consolidate the gains made during and up to the final resolution of the conflict. To this end, the activities of information and sensitization continued. These took the form of stand-alone designated meetings or sessions with the various parties who had been involved in the conflict. In addition, the various meetings of the different commissions and committees including the Good Office Commission, and the River Bani Committee, also brought together, not only the parties previously involved in the conflict, but also other locally elected officials, traditional leaders, youth and women organizations. These latter meetings provided opportunities for discussion on the management of the resources including land, water, and fishery. In effect, they helped to ensure that the resolution which they had agreed on continued to have the support of all the parties concerned.

This is because experience tells us that resolutions can come unstuck if one party feels that the letter or the spirit of the agreed upon resolution was not being respected.

The meetings, especially of the various committees, also served to keep the interested parties aware of the progress of the implementation and also helped to resolve any issues which might have had a negative effect on the Program. They worked to hold the parties together in a common bond aimed at ensuring that the waters of the Bani River flowed constantly for the benefit of all the riparian population. One of the committees had, as part of its mandate, the effective and efficient management of the different infrastructure developed under the Program. In the past, inadequate maintenance and inefficient management of the infrastructure in the rural areas and poor rainfall, had contributed to the reduction in productivity of crops and low level of production in the Program area.[2] These meetings served, to a large extent, as a monitoring mechanism managed by the people; the activities of the Program were thus, in effect, closely followed and observed. These factors positively influenced the duration of the implementation.

In addition to the sensitization and information sessions, other activities of the Program were being implemented even before the conflict was finally resolved. Table 5.1 shows that some of these activities in the Program were being implemented as part of the drive to achieve the objectives of the non-controversial components of the Programme. These included the development of the small irrigated perimeters such as the Tibi plain development works, works to rehabilitate the Diedala dam, and the construction of fifteen community health centers. Other activities carried out comprised the following: the realization of more than 70 kilometers of different types of irrigation canals, around 40 kilometers of dykes, four civil work structures, and the construction of large borehole wells. Many of these had been completed by mid 2004.

By 2006, 600 hectares had been developed, 1200 hectares had been put under rice cultivation, 200 farmers had received farming equipment, 156 had received fertilizers and chemical products and 134 kilometers of tracks had been constructed. The implementation of the dam construction works which were the object of the conflict started in April 2005 after the attribution of the contract in February 2005 and that of the road network in May 2005. The agricultural development works started in March 2007 after contract signing in January 2007.[3] By January 2007, the construction of the Talo Dam and the land development works on the targeted area had been completed. The Talo Dam was completed within two years. In the absence of the conflict, the dam would have been completed by 2002, according to the original schedule. The benefits of the Program would have been obtained earlier.

Apart from the physical realizations, some "soft" components were also being implemented during the suspension of the construction of the dam. These included the preparation of a directory of eighty existing farmer organizations and an evaluation of their operational performances. A total of 289 farmers from 10 farmer organizations received literacy classes, and 120 farmers, officials and trainers received training in various subjects. These included training in techniques of production, utilization of organic fertilization and seed selection. An aggregate number of 1300 women were made literate in the local languages and 370 women were given training in processing agricultural products into soap and also in cloth dyeing. By 2006, it was reported that ninety-nine village meetings and four community information meetings had been held. Other realizations concerned the livestock, fisheries, and aquaculture components.

The research component also saw some activities, with the development of 143 plots of land for the development and dissemination of improved seeds. Other research achievements included the finalization of the study on the lateral migration of fish and the establishment of consultative bodies for the discussion of issues relating to fisheries and aquaculture. The line of credit for the rural population was also set up and more than FCFA 46 million of the budgeted 50 million disbursed to twenty-one farmer organizations for the purchase of farming equipments and farming inputs. With regard to the environment, the environmental management plan, which was drawn up in 1998, was updated in 2003 and extended up to the town of Mopti in the north. An agreement was signed with the department of sanitation and fight against pollution and public nuisance of Mali for it to carry out situational analysis studies. Other studies carried out include the animal health epidemiological study. Forty-nine teachers were trained in environmental education and ecological sites were set up in eight primary schools. The construction of the Talo Dam had been completed by March 2007, and was opened by the president of the Republic in March of the same year.

The implementation went along, pari passu, with the monitoring activities which were carried out by both the AfDB and the Malian government. The monitoring activities by the AfDB included desk supervision as well as field supervision missions. It was reported that from 1998 to 2006, the Bank carried out twelve supervision missions. Counting from 1998, this comes to about 1.33 missions per year. This is more than the one supervision mission per year required by the AfDB Group, of the early 1990s, but less than the ratio of at least 1.5 supervision missions per year, prescribed later in the years 2000. Excluding 1998, which was the year during which no disbursement was expected, the ratio comes to 1.5. These missions, especially the ones carried out beginning in 2001, addressed both aspects of the technical implementation of the Program, and ensured that the information and sensitization campaign was being implemented satisfactorily. The number of staff per mission varied from one person to three persons, and the composition also varied. The mission composition depended generally on the major issue which the Program was encountering at the time of the supervision mission. From the program completion report it was observed that the principal officer in charge of the Program in the Bank was an irrigation engineer who participated in all supervision missions. Depending on the issue, the irrigation engineer would be accompanied by an agronomist or environmental specialist or a legal specialist. These missions produced supervision reports which formed part of the monitoring of the Program and also ensured that the required actions relating to such issues as the environmental plans, and the sensitization campaign were undertaken in time and followed through. The mission composition and number of mission members were influenced by many factors, not the least of which was the nature of issues or problems to be dealt with in the field.

It can be argued that for a program which had been the subject of a protracted conflict, the number of mission members and composition could have been strengthened, especially with the participation of a rural sociologist. This latter specialist however, was, available in the field as part of the program management team. The contribution from this specialist must have been integrated into the acceptable resolutions of the meetings and sessions, which were held as part of the conflict management process. On an ex post analysis such as the present, the various committees and commissions established as a result of the conflict, had communal stakes in the implementation and therefore provided a very robust supervision and monitoring mechanism.

Further monitoring of the Program was carried out by the Malian ministry of agriculture and rural development. The results of the implementation monitoring were consigned in the statutory reports which the Programme produced and submitted to both the ministry and the financiers. There were a total of fifty-six activity reports in all and six audit reports.

DISBURSEMENT

Disbursement is generally the responsibility of sector and finance departments in the AfDB as well as the relevant government departments in the countries concerned. The corresponding government department, generally the finance departments in the countries after receiving requests from the department implementing for the government concerned, forwards the requests to the financing institution. In this case, this was AfDB. In this section we will be concerned with disbursement schedules over the conflict and post conflict periods. These activities, in effect, represented over five years of implementation efforts. How did the conflict affect the disbursement of the loan?

Generally, disbursement procedures and process greatly influence implementation. The time taken to process disbursement requests through the sector and finance departments generally varies from a few days to several months depending on the work load of the departments concerned as well as their familiarity with the preparation and processing of disbursement requests, among other things. In addition, actual disbursement from the financing institution is also in part influenced, by the completeness of the request documentation, in terms of the accuracy of the completed forms. The supporting and justification documents provided and their completeness also influence the disbursement. The work load of the officers in the Bank, responsible for the program in the relevant sector department as well as the accounting and finance departments greatly influence the actual disbursement schedule.

The officers in the accounting and finance departments are responsible for processing the requests, ensuring the funds leave the account of the Bank and are entered into the account of the receiving government. In the present study, the original AfDF disbursement, ex ante was scheduled to commence in 1999 and terminate in 2002. From the reconstructed disbursement schedule, disbursement started in 1999 and ended in 2007. The actual disbursement amounts were far below the initially programmed amounts. In 1999, the actual disbursement amount, however, for the ADF was 5.4% of the initially programmed amount and 95.4% for the government disbursement. Disbursements in 2000 were supposed to be made for all three financiers, the AfDF, OPEC Fund and the government. Actual disbursement for the ADF however, was only 16.7% of the initially programmed amount, and that of the government was 100%. There was no disbursement from the OPEC fund. The original disbursement before the eruption of the conflict was to have been completed in 2002. In the reconstructed disbursement schedule, in 2002, only 45% of the initially programmed amount was actually disbursed and only 6.5% of the total loan funds had been disbursed.

The under-disbursement cannot all be attributed to the conflict, as even the scheduled amounts were not attained. This could possibly be attributed to the possible delays in either the submission or the processing of disbursement. It could also have been that the actual implementation rhythm was not as was programmed ex ante; or that the ex ante rhythm of implementation and the disbursement schedule were more optimistic than the reality was given to reflect on an ex post basis.

In the case of the OPEC Fund, the original disbursement was scheduled to start later than those of the AfDF and the government. Among the external financiers, the OPEC Fund was expected to finance only civil works, whereas the AfDF funds were to finance all components and all categories. Disbursement of AfDF funds was therefore more likely to be affected by any delay in implementation. Even so, because of the fact that the AfDF funds were to finance all categories, disbursement from these funds tended to take place even during the conflict period, as disbursement could be made for those non-controversial activities, as seen from Tables 5.3.

During the height of the conflict in the years 2000-2004, when no acceptable resolution seemed to be in sight, disbursement ranged from 17.7% to 45% of the initially programmed disbursement amounts for AfDF and 0% for disbursement from OPEC Funds. The reason for this was because the civil works constituted more than 65% of the total cost of the Program and around the same percentage of the total external funding. Disbursement of the funds provided by OPEC started only from 2005 when the conflict had been acceptably resolved, with 101% of the initially programmed amount being disbursed in 2005 and 98.84% disbursed in 2006. Disbursement from the AfDF funds also picked up in earnest in 2005 with 77.84% of the initially programmed amount being disbursed. In 2006 this increased to 90.84% and in 2007 51.16% of the initially programmed amounts were disbursed.

By December 2007, total disbursement had reached around 87% of the total loan amount. According to figures from the AfDB, as at March 2008, disbursement from the AfDF loan had reached around 95%; (Mali-Growth and Poverty Support Program-2008. Tables 5.3a, b, and c, illustrate the influence of the conflict and the time taken to resolve it on disbursement. It should be noted that according to the AfDF rules on disbursement, there were several disbursement methods. These include the revolving fund method whereby funds for operating cost for a specific period, often not exceeding six months, are made available to the programme implementing agency and these could be replenished when around 80% have been justifiably consumed. Other methods included direct payment to the approved contractor, consulting firm, or organization participating in the implementation of the Program.

All of these methods were used in the Program under study and contributed in some ways to the actual implementation and disbursement rhythm noted in Tables 5.3a, b and c. Given that contractors and others participating in the implementation of the Programme have to be recruited in accordance

Table 5.3a. Annual Disbursement Schedule, AfDB

Year	Disbursement Programmed	Disbursement Made	% of Programmed Disbursement Made	% Loan Disbursed
1999	Yes	Yes	5.4	0.57
2000	Yes	Yes	16.70	3.03
2001	Yes	Yes	17.70	1.3
2002	Yes	Yes	45.20	1.61
2003	Yes	Yes	18.30	4.00
2004	Yes	Yes	11.10	2.5
2005	Yes	Yes	77.80	30.30
2006	Yes	Yes	90.80	35.40
2007	Yes	Yes	51.16	4.50

Source: Adapted from Project Completion Report—Moyen Bani Program. African Development Bank

with set procedures, it can be argued that the pace of recruitment of implementing partners also influenced the rate of implementation and the tempo of disbursement. There is therefore a tendency for interdependence between disbursement tempo and implementation rate. There are instances however when contractors might self-finance implementation stages and request disbursement of funds to cover those stages later on in the course of the implementation schedule. In this way, implementation would be going on even though disbursements may not have been made. The precise amount of influence of these factors on both disbursement and implementation during the conflict and post conflict periods is not certain. For even the amount of disbursement on non-controversial activities showed some slackening in the pre-conflict and conflict periods. However, it is certain that the implementation and disbursement would have been completed much earlier than 2008 as was the case in the present Program.

Table 5.3b. Annual Disbursement Schedule, OPEC Fund

Year	Disbursement Programmed	Disbursement Made	% of Programmed Disbursement Made	% Loan Disbursed
1999	No	No	N/A	N/A
2000	Yes	No	N/A	N/A
2001	Yes	No	N/A	N/A
2002	No	No	N/A	N/A
2003	Yes	No	N/A	N/A
2004	No	No	N/A	N/A
2005	Yes	Yes	10.10	32.80
2006	Yes	Yes	98.90	46.70
2007	Yes	No	N/A	N/A

Source: Adapted from Project Completion Report—Moyen Bani Program. African Development Bank

Table 5.3c. Annual Disbursement Schedule, Government of Mali

Year	Disbursement Programmed	Disbursement Made	% of Programmed Disbursement Made	% Loan Disbursed
1999	Yes	Yes	95.4	12.10
2000	Yes	Yes	100.0	12.00
2001	Yes	Yes	23.00	4.50
2002	Yes	Yes	77.10	5.70
2003	Yes	Yes	48.20	10.70
2004	Yes	Yes	22.30	4.50
2005	Yes	Yes	92.50	14.40
2006	Yes	Yes	100.00	39.20
2007	Yes	Yes	93.80	16.70

Source: Adapted from Project Completion Report—Moyen Bani Program. African Development Bank

Another aspect which could have greatly influenced the post conflict disbursement and implementation rates is the increased scrutiny of the Program brought about by the various committees and commissions which were established to monitor the Program, as part of the final resolution of the conflict. These committees met regularly, under the chairmanship of the mediator. They acted as an added spur to implementation and disbursement, constantly monitoring activities of the Program, using indicators, and benchmarks along the programmed timeline of Program implementation.

Could it thus be argued that the conflict, even though it caused a delay in implementation, had some "beneficial" effect as it focused lots of attention on ensuring that the Program is completed effectively and efficiently? For one to surmise this would be to infer that without the conflict and without the increased focus consequent upon the conflict, the monitoring would not have been as intense as it was because of the conflict. Even though it cannot be denied that the conflict and the time taken to come to an acceptable resolution, increased attention on the Program and its implementation, the Program would have received due monitoring attention from both the AfDB and the government of Mali, given its importance to the Malian economy. In the final analysis, the argument of increased attention consequential upon all that caused and ensued from the conflict tends to be stronger. The president of the country had put his reputation at stake for the project as was seen earlier. The president of the AfDB, the executive directors of the AfDB were all concerned about the conflict resolution and the progress of the Program. All these made it possible to inject the high level of resources into monitoring and reporting activities concerning the Program. It would *not* be logical to assume from this that for programs to solicit high attention, it is necessary to inject a conflict into it. The conflict had taken its toll on resources.

A huge amount of resources have been expended towards the resolution of the conflict by the AfDB, by the Malian government, the Cultural Survival Organisation, the United States Agency for Development and possibly other organizations and bodies; resources which could have been utilized to further improve the economies of Mali and other regional member countries of the AfDB. These resources were expended on such items as person time for personnel of the various institutions and organizations involved in the conflict and conflict resolution. The remuneration of persons involved, including those of the mediator, cost of air and land travel into Mali as well as inside Mali. The cost of the various meetings should also be factored in the total cost. In addition, the conflict contributed to the delays in the production of many of the benefits of the Program. Quite apart from the benefits, it would be useful at this time, to review the effect of the conflict on the costs of the Program.

EFFECTS ON PROGRAM COSTS

In Chapter Three, the ex ante costs and breakdown of costs of the project were discussed. Here, it will be appropriate to see how those costs and cost items were affected by the conflict and the conflict resolution process. The total cost of the Program at the time of the analysis carried out for the Program completion report showed that the total cost had increased in terms of unit of account from UA26.89 million to UA 27.37 million, representing a 1.7% increase. In terms of CFA francs, there was a reduction in total cost between the initial appraisal and loan approval dates and the compilation of the Program completion report. The figures were FCFA 22,172.92 million at appraisal, and FCFA 21,445.11 million at preparation of the completion report, representing a 3.0% decrease.

In the AfDB, the accounts are held in units of accounts and in the Mali, the government contribution as well as the loan amounts are held in CFA francs. In effect, the changes in cost are calculated every year based on the local currency denomination equivalent of the unit of account. There therefore appeared, to have been an appreciation of the CFA francs in comparison with the unit of account. At appraisal in 1997 and loan approval in 1998, the exchange was 1UA= FCFA 824.698; at the preparation of Program completion report, in 2006, the exchange was 1UA= FCFA 782.501. This represented a 5% change. There were no supplementary loan given on this Program; the rates were readjusted, which accounted for the change in the UA equivalent. Can it be argued that this change in cost was caused by the conflict? There is no direct cause and effect between the conflict and the rate of exchange.

This is so, especially as the rate of exchange used in the operations of AfDF and AfDB, both of which make up the Bank Group, are regularly updated based on the relative strength of the various currencies used in international exchange and is the same as the special drawing rights of the International Monetary Fund. The exchange rates used in the Bank Group are fixed per quarter. Nevertheless, it can be argued that had the conflict not prolonged the implementation period of the Program, the final rate used would have been very different and might not have shown such a marked change in the cost of the individual components and the final total cost at the time of the preparation of the Program completion report.

The Program costs from a purely absolute value standpoint were greatly influenced by the reevaluation. The exchange rate between the Bank unit of account, in which the Program costs and the Program loan were recorded, and the CFA franc which was the national currency in which the country did its own accounting also influenced the final costs of the Program. As indicated earlier, the rate at Program appraisal was 1UA equal to CFA franc 824.698. At project completion, 1 UA was equal to CFA franc 782.501. Because of the appreciation of the CFA franc against the UA, the final absolute costs of the Program was 3.3% lower than the original cost in terms of CFA francs and 1.8% higher in terms of units of account. All of the components were affected as both local and foreign costs increased after the reevaluation with the major increase observed in the total cost of the land development works, which increased by around 17% in terms of francs and around 21% in terms of unit of account.[4]

THE CONFLICT, PROGRAM COSTS AND BENEFITS

The internal economic rate of return of the Program was calculated, ex ante, at 13% and the sensitivity analysis showed that the Programme was sensitive to a drop in returns more than it was to an increase in costs, with 11.1% and 12%, respectively. The differences in these figures do not appear to be very significant as compared with the 12.4% which would be the result of an increase in operating costs.[5] In the ex ante analysis, the consideration of an increase in cost, combined with a reduction in returns was not included. Ex ante analysis of a delay in the start-up of the implementation as well as in obtaining returns, was also not included in the final analysis. These latter analysis would have tested the sensitivity of the Programme to the type of issues that later bedeviled it.

Nevertheless, at Program completion, the ex post analysis, based on the same assumptions as for the ex ante analysis, showed that the internal economic rate of return was estimated at 16%. This is said to be higher than the opportunity cost of capital which was estimated at 12% at that time. What can be attributed to the improvement in the internal economic rate of return, in spite of the delay in the implementation of the major component caused by the conflict and the time taken to resolve it? Could the increased attention brought about by the conflict, have contributed to better implementation?

We will next examine the major factors which influence the economic rate of return. This could help ascertain which ones contributed to the positive difference in the ex ante and ex post rates of return of the Program. These factors comprise those which influence the returns, such as the yields, the area planted and harvested. They include the price of the final product and the spread of the returns over the period of the cost benefit analysis. In the same way, the spread of the major cost items over this period could also influence the rate of return. A longer spread of costs, especially if it is accompanied by some returns in the early years of the project could have a positive influence on the final rate of return. In the case of the Moyen Bani Program, the yields for paddy rice expected ex ante from the development of the land was around 2.5 metric tons per hectare as opposed to 0.9 metric tons per hectare under traditional cultivation system.[6] The yields actually obtained during the 2007–2008 season was 3.5 metric tons of paddy rice under controlled submersion system and 5 metric tons per hectare under complete submersion system.

These yields compare favorably with yields obtained under irrigation in such other projects as the Dakawa rice irrigation project in Tanzania (also financed by the AfDF) where the yield was at least 5 metric tons per hectare for paddy rice. They were also much higher than the ex ante yield of 2.5 metric tons per hectare.

The ex ante area programmed at full production was 4750 hectares of rice and 2470 hectares of fodder crop. In fact, the ex post areas cultivated in the first season, 2007–2008, were 1200 hectares under controlled submersion and 291 hectares under complete submersion, both of them for paddy. For the 2008–2009, the areas planted were 4,255 hectares for controlled submersion and 1,171 hectares under total submersion. For the 2009-2010 season the figures were 5,000 hectares and 800 hectares, respectively.[7] There were no ex post figures of yield or area cultivated for fodder crops. We see here, that both the yields and the areas cultivated were higher ex post than ex ante. This may have been because a larger cultivation area was made possible by the land development works. In addition, the major costs, which concerned the construction of the dam and the development of the land, were spread over a longer period as was seen earlier in the disbursement section. It could thus be argued that these contributed significantly to the positive difference between the ex ante and the ex post economic rates of return, especially under constant prices for the production. Thus, it can be observed that the conflict, directly and indirectly, had significant impact on both cost and benefits when one considers the ex post analysis which is part of the remit of the present study. What can therefore be concluded from the preceding chapters which had reviewed the Program in detail, ex ante as well as ex post?

NOTES

1. African Development Bank, Project Completion Report. Moyen Bani Program in Mali. http://www.afdb.org/fileadmin/uploads/afdb/Documents/Project-and-Operations/ Mali. Middle Bani Plains Development Programme _FR.pdf.

2. African Development Bank, Project Completion Report. Moyen Bani Program in Mali. Tunis. 2008.

3. African Development Bank, Project Completion Report. Moyen Bani Program in Mali. Tunis. 2008.

4. Analysis based on African Development Bank, Project Completion Report. Moyen Bani Program in Mali. Tunis. 2008.

5. African Development Bank, Appraisal Report. Moyen Bani Program in Mali. First Phase. Abidjan. 1998.

6. African Development Bank, Appraisal Report. Moyen Bani Program in Mali. First Phase. Abidjan 1998.

7. Analysis based on African Development Bank, Project Completion Report. Moyen Bani Program in Mali. Tunis. 2008.

Chapter Six

Conclusion

Mali is endowed with the River Niger and its tributaries which run through large swathes of its territory. These contributed and still contribute to making it a large producer of agricultural products, especially cereals and cotton. In addition, rainfall patterns, in the past significantly helped the production of crops. These positive results were nullified during the drought which affected the soudano-sahelian region in the 1970s and 1980s. The rainfall pattern deteriorated and the volume of water entering the rivers became seriously affected, leading, among other things, to a drop in the flow of water along their courses. This situation was aggravated in the 1980s and later by the persistence of the drought-like situation which prevented the rivers from recovering to their pre-drought levels.

During the same period from the 1980s through to the 1990s, the country went from being under military administration to one party rule and then to democratic government. This latter period brought out the teething troubles of a fledgling democracy, with student and civil unrest, multiplication of political parties and protests. All of these were compounded by poverty, slow development, and scarce foreign and domestic resources. Some of the protests during the early period of democracy in Mali were directed at government for not addressing the major issues related to reducing poverty.

It was in the desire to address these issues, to carry out the role expected of them, and also to score political kudos, that Malian governments, over the study period, designed development programs. The Moyen Bani Program was designed to address the specific problem of not having enough water flowing down the Bani River. This serious reduction in the flow of the river negatively affected the agricultural, fisheries and other economic activities and led to inadequacy of financial resources of the riparian population to meet their basic food and other needs.

The Program itself, designed to harness and to control the waters of the River Bani underwent several screening processes. These analyzed the area chosen for the dam to ensure its technical appropriateness and confirmed the technological justification of the selected method. They verified the cost aspects and ascertained the chances that the ex ante benefits and returns would be obtained ex post. In the bid to cater for all possible responses, the design of the Program endeavored to incorporate the various technical, social and economic factors which were expected to ensure success. Success, in the implementation, in the operation and in the attainment of the objectives was a key factor which informed the approval by the external financiers of the complementary funding required for the Program. Based on the studies and the observations of the various missions, all the possible reactions which the Program would elicit from the parties concerned and involved were factored into the design. Apart from a program document having all the necessary and relevant parameters for success, the program itself should be implementable and operational in reality, ex post.

In this regard, various complementary studies were carried out looking at different aspects of the Program. In addition, various missions from the financiers and the government visited the Program area and other relevant areas and had discussions with the population in the upstream and downstream areas of the dam. The mission members also had discussions and meetings with government officials, and members of the civil society in the attempt to gauge reactions, concerns and issues which could have consequences for the implementation and operations of the Program. Among these issues was the effect of the Program on the physical environment, especially the flow of the river to the downstream of the dam. This issue, which was thought to have been resolved, became the Achilles heel of the Program, the issue that was to make or break it. In fact, this issue nearly did break it, as it led to a protracted conflict which led to a suspension of the most important component of the Program, the construction of the dam, for more than six years.

The conflict was politicized and internationalized. This was done by the downstream population and their "advisers", in a bid to increase the political resources they had. By doing so they hoped it would ensure that their views receive very high priority. These views concerned mainly the assurance that there would be satisfactory quantities of water flowing downstream. They wanted satisfactory quantities which would not jeopardize their household and economic activities. The internationalization led to several instances of stalemate and "dialogue of the deaf", with neither side listening to the other, nor ready to review its position or frame. They tended to base their refusal or reluctance to modify their positions on their belief that they would succeed in getting their position accepted. Each party believed on the comparative strength of its case and the weakness of that of the opposing party. More particularly, in our view, they tended to believe on the strength of the political resources each party believed it had succeeded in obtaining.

The breakthrough came after the financiers agreed to break the impasse and carry out the complementary or additional studies which had been called for by the "advisers" of the downstream population. These studies ultimately led to the widening of the sluice gates among others. This widening of the sluice gates also assured the downstream population of the certainty that the volume of water flowing downstream, under the water control system, which the dam would introduce, would be adequate for their economic activities. In the process, the frames and perceptions of the downstream population changed several times. In addition, the downstream population was able to use their bargaining strength to ensure that they had a water control structure of their own in the vicinity of their major town, Djenne. This could be defined as a modification in the frames previously held by the parties concerned. They thus used a "bridging" strategy and negotiated a new option which helped to resolve the conflict. It was the acceptance of a new option in the conflict resolution process. It was a solution which assured each party that their potential settlement points would converge and move towards a more acceptable settlement. It ensured that the settlement area for both parties increased significantly. This achievement was aided by the mediator whose background contributed to arriving at the acceptable solution.

The relevance of perception, past experience, and emotions in defining frames in conflict cannot be over emphasized. It is also important to have a thorough insight into local beliefs and politics. All these factors played significant roles in the conflict and explained the different positions or frames held by the protagonists. The changes in frames by the parties concerned, between 2000 and 2005, had contributed to the protracted nature of the conflict. An assessment of local politics and beliefs by project preparation teams should be made and the results factored into the design of the project or catered for during implementation.

The external financiers and the central government were able to manage the pressure, subtle and in their eyes, imminently overt, successfully, although rather tardily. The sensitivity of the issues involved brought about the feeling among the upstream population, of external interference. They made this known in several of the meetings called to unravel the conflict. The downstream population could have countered by claiming a sense of justice and the necessity for this external involvement, this "triangulisation", to help make their case for increased flow of the river water and also attain a greater audience for their cause. They seemed to have appreciated the externalization and the conflict management process as these gave them not only voice, but also information. It helped them get a better understanding of the issues involved in the river flow as well as the issues concerning the dam and its construction. It also gave increased attention to their case as well as gave them increased participation in the affairs concerning the management of the structures built or those to be built on the River Bani. This could be confirmed by, among others, the numerous information and sensitization sessions they had with the technical teams from the external financiers, from the government and with the mediator.

In the end, the answer to the question as to whether the externalization should be considered as external assistance or external interference in the affairs of Mali, the scale tended, in this particular case, to weigh more in favor of the external interference being a positive factor for the downstream population. However, it was negative for the upstream population, as it delayed the program benefits for them. Nevertheless, it also tended to contribute to improved monitoring and greater chances of concrete results and positive impact of the Program on the life and wellbeing of the population concerned, both upstream and downstream, as well as for the Malian economy.

Can we then conclude that all development programs should have conflicts and go through conflict resolution processes as well as external interference/assistance in their implementation or operation? This position could be untenable, because conflicts could be divisive and could hinder development and progress, especially if not handled and resolved with skill. An external "eye" on the program, could also lead to calls of interference, which may have a negative effect on implementation. The fact that there are external financiers could be considered as having an "external eye or eyes" on the program.

Nevertheless, one can conclude, from the preceding analysis, that it is essential and critical for all participants in a development program to be given all the relevant information and they should participate in the various fora and "question and answer" sessions concerning the program, during program preparation. This would ensure that the frames they develop of the project would be harmonized and synchronized before implementation starts. The mission members involved with the preparation of the Moyen Bani Program did that ex ante as well during the conflict. With the wisdom of hindsight, however, this did not seem to have been enough to avoid the conflict which ensued. Nevertheless, it could be argued that the processes which the conflict resolution triggered could help in future programs, especially when they are carried out ex ante. The results obtained ex post could not all be attributed to the external "eye." The organizations, groups, committees, and commissions set up as part of the initial design of the programme and also those which were set up as part of the conflict resolution process contributed in a significant way to the results. These created, as it were, national and local "eyes" on the implementation and the operations of the program.

The issue of an international "eye" would not be relevant and necessary if the design of the program is solid and robust and the national and local "eyes" are thorough, in both their implicit or explicit oversight. In addition, the management team should be skilful, effective, efficient, rigorous, and thorough. In these circumstances, the external "eye," whether from the external financier or from one of the non-governmental organizations would be superfluous. Nevertheless, it would be worthwhile to explore further, the effect of increased international publicity on a development program of a country. Such a study could look at the monitoring, implementation, avoidance of conflict, and eventual success or failure of the project in meeting its objectives.

The analysis of the conflict and conflict resolution process brought to light the specific issue of what we could term "reflective timing." This relates to the precise point in a conflict at which each party should sit down and seriously discuss intra-murally the strength of the political and/or economic resources it is counting on to win. The discussion should also include assessment of whether these resources would effectively provide them with what is necessary to attain their objective as against those of the other party. The conflict and conflict resolution process also raised national awareness of the Program. This contributed to the increased attention and monitoring of the Program, during and after the conflict period. There were components and activities, though, which were carried out during the conflict period which were not affected by the conflict. These contributed to the positive results obtained in the ex post analysis, especially as some returns were being obtained, even though such major items, as the water control structure, the irrigation and land development works had not yet started.

It could also be argued that these results and the delay in the construction of the dam, helped to spread out the cost and returns over several years. This was done in such a way that over the cost-benefit analysis period used by the project completion report preparation team, the accumulation of major investment costs over the period was not very pronounced. This can be compared to what it would have been, if all the investment costs had been located in the early years of program implementation, when there would have been little or no returns. The "soft" components, such as training in raw material processing, the information and education activities, the establishment of groups and the training of these groups, were all positive factors which contributed to the final results of and return to the Program, ex post. These were greatly aided by the strong rhythm of disbursement on and implementation of some components, especially the major ones. These, in many instances were carried out within short turn-around periods.

In the final analysis, the strong interaction of politics, public administration, and agricultural development led, in this particular case, to a conflict. The combination of politics, public administration, agricultural development, and conflict seemed to have had, for a time, a paralyzing influence on the country's agricultural development. The intervention of conflict management and conflict resolution into the public administration of agricultural development, in this particular case, had as an underlying cause, a breakdown in communication among the relevant actors and participants of the Moyen Bani Program. This paralyzing influence actually and significantly constrained implementation activities for a very long period. In fact, from some of the literature on conflict resolution, referred to in the notes to the chapters, there tended to be very negative results from the type of interaction mentioned earlier, both in developing countries as well as in developed countries. Spencer had shown how such breakdown in communication and the interaction of politics, public administration and agricultural development could lead to disastrous effect on agricultural development.[1] The case of the Moyen Bani Program confirmed that certain prerequisites, such as full step by step involvement of those concerned and involved with the program and the diffusing of relevant information, could help to avoid conflicts and communication breakdowns in development programs. We could reiterate the need for a thorough review of the local politics, beliefs, and perceptions on development of the target population. A case could also be made for the early involvement of a mediator in the conflict resolution process, before the conflict becomes intractable.

This analysis revealed that development programs, in developing countries, especially major programs as defined by total cost, and in particular, programs in the rural development area, tended to have more than their fair share of "international or external eye." This is true, especially if one takes into account the very large number of international NGOs which make developing countries their terrain of intervention and rural development their area of predilection. This could cause promoters of such programs and their financiers to be constantly "looking over their shoulders." It could also cause them, or perhaps help them, to be much more rigorous and thorough in their ex ante analysis of the programs and more flexible and alert in the implementation and management. This should mean a more detailed and far sighted examination of the reactions and responses which the programs would elicit. It would also mean an examination of the motivation underlying these reactions, identifying factors which enter into the motivational equations. It would mean more willingness to review, revisit and modify program parameters in the course of implementation. This is an approach which some major international financial institutions are beginning to espouse.

It would be worthwhile if such factors would be examined from the sociological, psychological, historical and especially, the political standpoints. They should also be thoroughly reviewed from the standpoint of what Hirshleifer[2] would term, the "dark side of the economic forces," the desire to acquire more resources from a set pool to the detriment of the other party, in a mutual malevolent setting. This thus reduces the potential settlement region. All of this would ensure that the probability of conflicts is reduced. It is very likely that it would also lead to modifications in the original design of the initial programme. Consequently, this could be considered a further confirmation of the case for satisfactory lead time in project cycle development prior to start of the expected program implementation, factoring, among others, satisfactory start up time for contractors and consultants. Start-up time should be understood as that time necessary for contractors and consultants to set their machinery and staff in place on the site and in motion. It also encourages more in-depth analysis of recently executed development programs to ascertain factors which had influenced their success or failure. The economies of developing countries would gain significantly from such analysis and would provide a set of concrete empirical evidence to assist the analysis, the planning, the preparation and the management of projects. It would help identify potential conflict settings during project planning and design. It would also contribute towards improving conflict aversion strategies. Such an analysis would also contribute to the body of knowledge to help researchers in identifying factors which are positive to successful implementation over several programmes within the same geographical area or within the same sub-sector.

It is imperative that all efforts are always made, as in this particular conflict, to ensure that a peaceful resolution of a conflict is arrived at and an agreement acceptable to all parties is reached. Such an agreement should ensure that no party feels that its feelings have been hurt, its beliefs and traditions disrespected, or that it has lost "face." This is critical in order to prevent such inter community conflicts leading to physical violence and/or latent national conflict which can be ignited later on to the detriment of efforts at reducing poverty and enhancing sustainable development.

The question can be legitimately asked as to whether it is really possible to anticipate and prepare for *all* possible reactions and responses a program would elicit. It would be simplistic to believe that one could do so. However, it would be appropriate that for those reactions and responses which could be anticipated, the corrective, mitigating or nullifying mechanisms and/or measures should be incorporated into the design of the program. For those which cannot be foreseen or anticipated, it would be necessary and prudent to build contingency factors, with probable and extensive sensitivity analysis into the design. These would contribute towards ensuring that in all ways, the design of the program is robust enough to cater for such eventualities as political wrangling and possible conflict, before and during implementation. As was indicated earlier, it would be judicious if management would be willing to revisit the programme parameters and modify them as necessary during programme implementation.

NOTES

1. Chuku-Dinka R. SPENCER, "Politics, Public Administration and Agricultural Development: A Case Study of the Sierra Leone Industrial Plantation Development Program, 1964–1967." *The Journal of Developing Areas*. 12 (1). October 1977. Pp 82–84.

2. Jack HIRSHLEIFER, "The Dark Side of the Force. Economic Foundations of Conflict Theory." Cambridge: Cambridge University Press. 2001. p 30.

Bibliography

Adam Smith Institute. "Corporate Governance Developments and Implications for the African Development Bank." May 2003. OPSD.
African Business. Article: "ADB Long-term Credit Rating raised to AAA," from African Development Bank Newsletter, High beam Research. May1, 2004. At: www.highbeam.com/doc/1G1-117180389.html.
African Development Bank. Mali. Appraisal Report of the Moyen Bani Program. 1998. Also www.riob.fr/IMG/pdf/Atelir_Dakar_BANIDef.pdf.
———. Environmental Impact Assessment Summary. Mali-Moyen Bani Program. 1998.
———. Feasibility Study. Mali. Moyen Bani Program. 1988.
———. Ghana Forestry Project. April 2002.
———. "Independent Review Mechanism." At: www.afdb.org/en/about-us/structure/independent-review-mech.
———. "Information Note on Talo Dam in Mali''. 2003.
———. Project Completion Report. Moyen Bani Program in Mali. December 2007. http://www.afdb.org/fileadmin/uploads/afdb/Documents/Project-and-Operations/Mali. Middle Bani Plains Development Programme _FR.pdf.
———. "Proposal for a Supplementary Loan: Growth and Poverty Reduction Strategy Support Program." 2008. At: www.afdb.org/fileadmin/uploads/afdb/Documents/Project-and-Operations/Mali—Growth and Poverty Reduction Strategy Support Program (GPRSSP) and assist in Mitigating the Impact of the Global Crisis.pdf.
African Economic Outlook. "Mali- Country Statistics."
Agricultural Bulletin Board on Data Collection, Dissemination and Quality of Statistics FCPMIS. "Mali- Statistics on Cereal."
ALAO, Abiodun. "Natural Resources and Conflict in Africa. The Tragedy of Endowment." Rochester: University of Rochester Press. 2007.
ALLAM, Mahmood. "Problems and Potentials of Irrigated Agriculture in Sub-Saharan Africa." in *Journal of Irrigation and Drainage Engineering*. 117(2). Technical Papers. Pp 155–172. March/April 1991. American Society of Civil Engineers.

Applied Language. "Economy of Mali." At: www.appliedlanguage.com.
Association for Conflict Resolution. "Frequently Asked Questions" At: www.acrnet.org/about/CR-FAQ.htm.
AUGSBURGER, David W. "Conflict Mediation Across Cultures. Pathways and Patterns." Louisville. London: Westminster John Knox Press. 1992.
AVRUCH, Kevin. "Culture and Conflict Resolution." Washington, D.C. United States Institute of Peace. 1998.
Bank Information Center. "World Bank Urged to Postpone Loan for Controversial Gold Mine in Ghana"- January 30, 2006. At: www.bicusa.org/en/article.2611.aspx.
BBC- "Web Campaign against Ethiopia Dam." BBC News. March 23, 2010. At: www.newsvbote.bbc.co.uk.
BARBANTI, Olympio jr. "Development and Conflict Theory." "Beyond Intractability." August 2004. p 2. www.beyondintractibilty.org/essay/development.
BASSEY, Celestine Oyom and OSHITA, Oshita, O. Eds. "Conflict Resolution, Identity Crisis and Development in Africa." Lagos, Oxford, Benin: Malthouse Press Ltd. Abuja: Institute of Peace and Conflict Resolution. 2007.
BLAIR, Jeff. "Ethnic and National Identity in Africa: Lessons and Resources on Africa." World Affairs Council. The Seattle Foundation.
BLANKENSHIP, Erin. "Kashmiri Water: Good Enough for Peace." In Pugwash on line- Conferences on Science and World Affairs.
BOWMAN, Adam. "How Different Are Our Perceptions?" Ohio Conflict Solutions. Blog posted on May 27-2010. At: www.ohioconflictsolutions.com/blogg/how-different-are-our-perceptions.
BROCK-UTNE, Birgit. "Peace Research with a Diversity Perspective: A look at Africa" in *The International Journal of Peace Studies*. 9(2). Autumn/Winter 2004.
———. "Indigenous Conflict Resolution in Africa"—a draft presented to the Weekend Seminar on Indigenous Solutions to Conflict Resolution. Institute for Educational Research. University of Oslo- February 23-24, 2001.
BURGESS, Guy, and BURGESS, Heidi. "Environmental Mediation: Beyond the Limits Applying Dispute Resolution Principles to Intractable Environmental Conflicts" Conflict Research Consortium. Working Paper 94-50 February 1994.
BUSH, Robert A. Baruch, and BINGHAM, Lisa Blomgren. "The Knowledge Gaps Study: Unfinished Work, Open Questions" in *Conflict Resolution Quarterly*. 23(1). Fall 2005.
CANTOR, Paul. "Getting the Board of Directors on Board." In IVEY Business Journal- Improving the Practice of Management- Report # 9B03TA02. January/February 2003.
CASON, Jim. "Africa: Controversy Continues to dog Major World Bank Project" In CORPWATCH. April 25-2002. www.corpwatch.org/article.php?id=2410.
CHARNOVITZ, S. "Accountability of Non-governmental Organizations (NGO's) In "Global Governance." The George Washington University Law School, Public Law and Legal Theory. Working Papers. April 2005.
CHILDS, Larry. "Talo Dam Construction Delay Holds: African Development Bank and Malian Government Implement Cultural Survival Recommendations." *Cultural Survival Quarterly*. 28(1). March 15, 2004.

Christian Reformed Church, Office du Niger. OSJ. www.crcna.org/pages/office duniger.cfm.
CLARK University, "Report on the Talo Dam in Mali." See www.clarku.edu and also www.culturalsurvival.org.
COHEN, Raymond. "International Communication in an Interdependent World. Negotiating across Cultures." Revised edition. Washington, D.C. United States Institute of Peace Press. 1997.
COSER, Lewis. "Functions of Social Conflict: An Examination of the Concept of Social Conflict and Its Use in Empirical Sociological Research." New York: Free Press. 1956.
COULIBALY, M. and SISSOKO, A. "Inauguration du Seuil de Talo: Que de Chemin Parcouru." L'Essor. No. 15916 of 2007-03-19.
DAVIS, Andrea. "On the Rocks: The African Development Bank Struggles to stay afloat." July 1, 1996. Multinational Monitor. www.allbusiness.com/speciality-business/581033-1.html.
de JORIO, Rosa. "Narrative of the National Democracy in Mali." In 'Cahiers d'Etudes Africaines, 172-2003. March 02, 2007.
Demdigest. "Indonesia: external support for Local Democracy Agenda" in *Democracy Digest*. At: www.demdigest.net/blog/970/indonesia-external-support-local-democracy-agen.
DENG, Francis. "Anatomy of Conflict in Africa" in VAN de GOOR, Luc, RUPESINGHE, Kumar, and SCIARONE, Paul, Eds. "Between Development and Destruction: An Enquiry in the Causes of Conflict in Post Colonial State." The Netherlands Ministry of Foreign Affairs (DGIS) in association with The Netherlands Institute of International Relations, CLINGENDAEL. The Hague. 1996.
d'ENTREMONT, Deidre. "The Djenne Project, Mali". Jean Louis Bourgeois, Coordinator. *Cultural Survival Quarterly*. 25(2). July 31, 2001. p 2.
DIA, C.A. "3ieme Session du Conseil de Surveillance du PMB: Après la Persuasion, la mise a exécution." L'Essor.- 2002-02-13.
———. "Projet Moyen Bani: "Le Seuil de Talo sort de la controverse." L'Essor-No. 15193- 2004-04-27.
DIALLO, A.O. "Développement de l'Afrique: la BAD en première ligne." L'Essor no. 16039 of 2007-09-25.
DIARA, Souleymane et al. "Decentralization in Mali: Putting Politics into Practice." Bulletin # 362, Series: Decentralization and Local Governance. HILHORST, Thea and BALTISSEN, Gerard, Eds. SNV Mali. Royal Tropical Institute (KIT)- Amsterdam. KIT Development, Policy and Practice. 2004.
DIFFIN, Elizabeth. "Can our brain help us solve conflicts?" BBC News Magazine. March 11, 2010. At: www bbc.co.uk/2/hi/uk_news/.../8562008.stm.
DJENNE INITIATIVE, "International Human Rights, Cultural and Environmental Advocacy." - www.djenneinitiative.org.
DJENNE PATRIMOINE, "The Talo Dam." - http://Djenne-patrimoine.fr/racine/dp19htm.
DOYLE, Mark. "Campaigners Urge US and Europe to Cut Cotton Subsidies." BBC News Africa. November 14, 2010.

Drymon. "Drought Monitoring and Yield Forecasting." Drought Monitoring in Mali- 1997–1999– SCATMALI. At: www.neo.nl.

Economic and Social Council. United Nations Organization Committee on NGOs 17th and 18th Meeting, "Non-governmental Committee Recommends 32 Civil Society Groups for Consultative Status with Economic and Social Council. 29 May 2008."

ENGEL, Antonia and KORF, Benedikt. "Negotiation and Mediation Techniques for Natural Resource Management." Rome: Food and Agriculture Organization of the United Nations. Rome 2005.

ESSOR Newspaper, no. 15193 of 2004-04-27… See also www.essor.gov.ml.

European Commission. "Are There Too Many Players in the Field of External Assistance." In "Europe Aid."

"Fairtrade Foundation report reveals $47 billion subsidies locking West African Farmers in Poverty." November 2010. At: www.fairtrade.org.uk/press_office/press_releases_and_statements/november/fairtrade_foundation_report_reveals_47_billion_subsidies_locking_west_african_farmers_in_poverty.aspx.

FAO. "Cotton Commodity Notes." www.fao.org/es/esc/en.15/304/highlight_307.html Rome: FAO.

———. "Irrigation Potential in Africa: A Basin Approach." *Land and Water Bulletin* No.4. Rome: FAO 1997.

FISHER, Roger, URY, William, and PATTON, Bruce. "Getting to Yes. Negotiating Agreement without Giving In." Second edition. New York: Penguin Books. 1991.

FISHER, William, MEIEROTTO, Lisa, and RUSSEL, Ryan. "The Talo Dam Project: Projet de Mise en Valeur des Plaines en Moyen Bani." April 26, 2002. In Dialogue Between Nations. At: www.dialoguebetweennations.com.

Freedom House. "Freedom in the World- Mali" (2006). At: www.freedomhouse.org/inc/content.pubs/tiw/inc_country_detail.cfm?year=2006.

Friends of the Earth. "World Bank and Fossil Fuel." At: www.foe.org/international-work/world-bank-background.

Geographic- "Data on Mali" www.geographic.org.

GLEICK, Peter. "International Water Resources", Chapter Two, Sections 2.2 and 2.3.1. CA and CC Press. Sweden. AB Publishing House.

———. "Water and Conflict: Freshwater Resources and International Security" In 'International Security', 18 (1). Summer 1993.

GRAY, Barbara. "Framing of Environmental Disputes" In LEWICKI, Roy, GRAY, Barbara, and ELLIOTT, Michael, Eds. "Making Sense of Environmental Conflicts. Concepts and Cases." Washington, D.C. Covelo. London: Island Press. 2003.

GRESTE, Peter. "Ethiopia dam could spark water wars"- BBC News Africa. March 26, 2009. At: http://news.bbc.co.uk/2/hi/africa/7959814.stm.

HIRSHLEIFER, Jack. "The Dark side of the Force. Economic Foundations of Conflict Theory." Cambridge: Cambridge University Press. 2001.

HOCHET, Peter. "Institutional Choices and Local Custom in Minyankala, Southern Mali." May 28, 2006. Paper submitted to the Conference of the International Association for the Study of Common Property in Bali.

HUMPHRIS, Phillip. "Nargis and Beyond: a choice between sensationalism and political inaction?" In Humanitarian Exchange Magazine.- Humanitarian Practice Network. Overseas Development Institute. Issue 41. December 2008. At: www.odihpn.org/report.asp?ID=2967.

INA-SA-"Cotton-Producing-Countries" at www.ina.gr/cotton_producing_countries.htm.

International Monetary Fund. IMF Data-www.imf.org/external/pubs/ft/scr/2000/cr00126.pdf.

———. Article IV Consultations with Mali- "Selected Economic Indicators."

International Water Management Institute. "Investment in Agricultural Water Management in Sub Saharan Africa: Diagnosis of Trends and Opportunities." Theme Studies Report. September 30, 2004. IWMI-CGIAR.

IMPERATO, Pascal James. "Mali. A Search for Direction." Boulder and San Francisco, Dartmouth, and London. Westview Press, 1989.

IROBI, Edwin Godwin. "Ethnic Conflict Management in Africa: A comparative Case Study of Nigeria and South Africa." In "Annotated Conflict Cases." Conflict Resolution Information Sources. May 2005. CRInfo.

KIKUCH, M, INOCENCIO, A, TONOSAKI, M, MERREY, D, deJONG, and I, SALLY, H. "Cost of Irrigation Projects: A Comparison of Sub-Saharan Africa and Other Developing Regions and Finding Options to Reduce Costs." IWMI Research Report-109. IWMI.

KUKK, Christopher L, and DEESE, David A. "At the Water Edge: Regional Conflicts and Cooperation over Fresh Water." UCLA *Journal of International Law and Foreign Affairs*. Spring 1996.

LANEK, Richard. "Traditional Approaches among the Acholis in Northern Uganda." Paper presented at the All Africa Conference on African Principles of Conflict Resolution and Reconciliation. Addis Ababa, Ethiopia. November 1999.

LEWICKI, Roy and GRAY, Barbara. "Introduction" In LEWICKI, Roy, GRAY, Barbara and ELLIOTT, Michael, Eds. "Making Sense of Intractable Environmental Conflicts. Concepts and Cases." Washington, D.C. Island Press. 2003.

Malikounda-2006-09-18, "Développement du Bassin du Bani: feu vert pour le PDRI/Djenne" at www.malikounda.com/nouvelle_voir.php?id/Nouvelles.

MALLABY, Sebastian. "NGO's Fighting Poverty, Hurting the Poor" in "Foreign Policy." September 1, 2004.

MALTHUS, Thomas. "An Essay on the Principle of Population," Library of Economics and Liberty: http://www.econlib.org/library/Malthus/malPlong.html. Book I.II.1-9.

MANSA Newsletter. "The Talo Dam Project in Mali." No. 45. Winter 2000–2001.

MATCL. Ministère de l'Administration Territoriales et des Collectivités Locales MATCL- "Partis Politiques." Bamako. Government of Mali.

MIALL, Hugh. "The Peace-Makers: Peaceful Settlements of Disputes since 1945." London: MacMillan. 1992.

MINGST, Karen A. "Politics and the African Development Bank." Lexington, Kentucky: University Press of Kentucky. 1990.

NICHOLSON, Michael. "Conflict Analysis." London: English University Press, 1970. And New York: Barnes & Noble Inc. 1971.

NYONG, Anthony. "Climate Related Conflicts in West Africa." In "Population, Health, Environment and Conflict." ESCP. Report Issue 12.

OLYMPIC NEWS at: www.Insidethegame.com/Olympics/OlympicsNews. London. 18–19 October 2009.

PETRILLO, Justine. "Cultural Survival Endorses Revised Plan for Talo Dam Construction." *Cultural Survival Quarterly*. 28(3). September 15, 2004.

PHOTIUS. "Mali-Economy" at www.photius.com/wfb199/mali/mali_economy.html.

RUBIN, J, PRUIT, D. and KIM, S. "Social Conflict: Escalation, Stalemate, and Settlement." Second edition. New York: McGraw-Hill. 1994.

SANDY, Matt. "Blair's Guru's daughter loses Fight for Safe seat." at Daily Mail on line May18, 2009: http://www.dailymail.co.uk/news/article-1183455/Blair-gurus-girl-Georgia-Gould-22-loses-fight-safe-seat.html.

SHAH, Anup. "Non-governmental Organizations on Development Issues." In *Global Issues*. June 1, 2005. www.globalissues.org/article/25/non-governmental-organization.

SOMADO, E., GUEI, R, and NGUYEN, N. "Overview: Rice in Africa." Bouake: WARDA. 2008.

SPENCER, Chuku-Dinka R. "Politics, Public Administration, and Agricultural Development: A Case study of the Sierra Leone Industrial Plantation Development Program, 1964–67." *The Journal of Developing Areas.* 12(1). October 1977. Published by the Western Illinois University, Macomb, Illinois.

SUNDAR, Pushpar. "He who Pays the Piper: Funding Sources and NGO Credibility: An Indian Perspective." Indian Centre for Philanthropy, Sector - C, July 11–14, 2004.

http://atlas-conferences.com/c/a/l/l/10.htm.

SUSSKIND, Lawrence and CRUIKSHANK, Jeffrey. "Breaking the Impasse. Consensual Approaches to Resolving Public Disputes." New York: Basic Books, Inc. 1987.

TOURE, Brehima. "Mali, barrage de la discorde" in Syfia-Mali. 01-02-1999. www.syfiainfoindex.php.5?view&action&idArticle=502.

UNCTAD. www.unctad.org/sections/dite_fdistat/docs/wid_cp_ml_en.pdf.

United Nations Economic Commission for Africa. See www.uneca.org/aisi/nici/country_profiles/mali/malinter.htm.

8th World Wilderness Congress. Resolution #16. September 30–October 6, 2005. Anchorage, Alaska.

WARNER, Michael. "Conflict Management in Community-Based Natural Resource Projects: Experiences from Fiji and Papua New Guinea." Working Paper 135. Overseas Development Institute Research Papers. April 2000.

WATKINS, Thayer. "Office du Niger and the Scheme to Irrigate the Sahara Desert." At Applet-Magic.com.

Web-Atlas. "Water, Source of Tension." Web-Atlas on Regional Integration in West Africa. At: www.atlas-ouestafrique.org.

WEITZMAN, Eben A. and WEITZMAN, Patricia Flynn. "Problem Solving and Decision Making in Conflict Resolution." In "The Handbook of Conflict Resolution: Theory and Practice." San Francisco: Jossey-Bass Publishers. 2000. Pp 185–209.

World Bank Group. "Mali at a Glance." September 24, 2008. At www.worldbank.org.

———. Country Profile-Mali- Data profile. At: http://ddp-ext.worldbank.org/ext/ddpreports/ViewSharedReport?/R.

———. http://ddp-ext.worldbnk.org/ext/ddpreports/ViewSharedReport?R.

———. Mali-World Development Indicators database. April 2009.

World Trade Organization (WTO). Report of the African Regional Workshop on Cotton, Cotonou, Republic of Benin—March 23–24, 2004.

Index

Abacha, Sani, 27
ADEMA. *See* Alliance pour la Democratie au Mali
AfDB. *See* African Development Bank
AfDB Group, 83
AfDF. *See* African Development Fund
African Development Bank (AfDB), 5; conflict resolution concern of, 88; C.S. letter to, 50–51; decisions in 2003, 60–61; disbursement by, 84–89; history of, 26; monitoring by, 83–84; 1970s compared to 1990s, 53; non regional members in, 25–26; preparation stage importance to, 22–23; procurement suspended by, 50; public image and rating of, 55–56, 59; water flow issue reversion by, 54. *See also* funding
African Development Fund (AfDF), annual disbursement from, *87*
agriculture, 10–11; economy of 1990s and, 13–14, *15*, *16*, *17*; Program goal of increased production, 28–29; yields and, 21, 91. *See also* hydro-agricultural civil works
Alliance pour la Democratie au Mali (ADEMA), 12
AND. *See* Association of Natives of Djenne

Anikulapo-Kuti, Fela, 27
annexation, by France, 9
appraisal report, 22–29, 35–36, 50; screening processes for, 24–25; sector goal in, 28–29; Talo dam objectives in, 30, *30*, 33
Association of Natives of Djenne (AND), 5, 62; conflict "triangulisation" by, 49–50, 51, 95–96; Cultural Survival coalition with Djenne population and, 49–50, 51; Djenne people's disparity with, 67; intervention of, 46; management team recourse of, 35; NGO as uninvited adviser for, 69; upstream people's mistrust of, 58–59

Bani River, 3, 21
Bani River Basin Management Committee, 60, 61–62, 81
borgou, 29
bridging, 62, 95

central government, 9–10; as Borrower, 36; downstream population in conflict with, 47, 48; election oversight responsibility of, 47; external funding solicitation by, 3; meetings with dignitary of, 62; upstream population and, 58

cereals: deficit, 28; harvest and production 1990-2000, *15, 16*; production in million metric tonnes 1990-2000, *17*
CGIAR. *See* Consultative Group on International Agricultural Research
China, 74
civil works, 35, 79–80; cost of, 31–32; hydro-agricultural, 31, *33*, 34; implementation of, *80, 81*
Clark University, 68, 69
communes, decentralization through, 13–14
Comparative Irrigation Cost Study, 32
complementarity, moderate, 45
complementary studies, 53–54, 63, 65, 94
conflicts: analyses of, 6; definition of, 43–45; delays caused by, 5; disputes distinguished from, 44; framing of, 41, 52; media role in, 47; NGO publicizing of, 52–53, 63, 69–70, 71, 74–75; resource, 5, 43–46, 68–69; sources of, 1
conflict, Program: beginning of, 46–49; breakthrough in, 60–65; conflict management, 53–56, 64; costs and benefits, 90–92; crux of, 5; C.S. understanding of, 72; delay caused by, 38, 65, 94; disbursement during, 86; as distributional, 54, 55; EIAS and, 18, 24, 38–40, 53–54, 60; epilogue, 64; externalization of, 49–53, 67–75, 95–96; impasse in, 57–58; implemented activities during, 82–83; increased monitoring and attention due to, 88; international publicity on, 94–95, 96–97, 98; intractability of, 55–56, 59–60, 66, 74; management of, 53–56, 64; as politicized, 5, 62, 66, 94–95; Program cost impacted by, 89–90; technical issues, 3–4, 62–63, 68; "triangulisation" of, 49–50, 51, 95–96; under-disbursement due to, 85–86. *See also* mediator; post-conflict period
conflict resolution: AfDB concern with, 88; agreeable to all parties, 99; assessment of, 65–67; benevolent intentions and, 45; bridging as, 62, 95; costs associated with, 89; factors enhancing, 65–66; in traditional cultures, 47–48, 49, 56, 68, 71
constitutional rights, 44
construction, 79–81, *80*, 82; completion of dam, 82; delayed, 94
Consultative Group on International Agricultural Research (CGIAR), 32, 33
consulting firm, 23
corner stone ceremonial, 64
corrective measures, 40
costs, 31–34, *33*; conflict resolution impact on total, 89; costs and benefits of conflict, 90–92; final, 81; foreign exchange rates and, 33, 89–90; longer spread of, 91, 97; monitoring, 88, 89; sunk, 47; total cost calculations, 32–33
cotton, 14
C.S. *See* Cultural Survival
Cultural Survival (C.S.), 5, 38, 70; absence from tripartite meeting, 57, 72; AfDF and, 34; coalition between AND, Djenne population and, 49–50, 51; conflict intractability and, 74; conflict understood by, 72; Djenne dam viewed by, 62; externalization through, 49–53; letter to AfDF, 50–51; as low-context culture, 51, 71, 72; positive impact of intervention by, 74; publicizing of conflict by, 52–53, 63, 71, 74–75; rural development perceptions of, 71; web site of, 52–53, 63
culture: C.S. as low-context, 51, 71, 72; high-context, 47–48, 49, 51, 53, 56, 72

dams, 28, 74; Djenne-level, 62, 63; downstream effects of, 39, 41; size classification of, 33. *See also* Moyen Bani Program; Talo dam
decentralization, 12–14, 47
democracy, 93
development finance institutions (DFIs), 54–55; USAID, 53, 63, 68
development projects, 69; conflict sources in, 1; external funding solicitation for, 3; government-funded, 31; international publicity on, 94–95, 96–97, 98; preparation procedures for, 4–5; third sector in, 70. *See also* rural development projects
DFIs. *See* development finance institutions
disbursement, funding, 84–89; annual schedule of, *87*; during conflict, 86; under-, 85–86
displacement, 49, 69
disputes, conflicts distinguished from, 44
distributional conflict, 54, 55
Djenne, mosque in, 51
Djenne Forum, 58
Djenne people: coalition between AND, C.S. and, 49–50, 51; conflict issues taken up by, 47; dignity and honor restored to, 64; AND disparity with, 67; downstream effects on, 41; perceptions of, 41; separate dam for, 62, 63; water flow concern of, 52
downstream effects, 39, 41
downstream population: conflict parties as central government and, 47, 48; EIAS issues for, 18, 24, 40; ethnicity and culture of, 51; externalization response, 95–96; tension between upstream and, 56
drought, 1970s and 1980s, 12, 21, 59, 93

economic and financial analysis, of Program, 37–38

economic rate of return (ERR), sensitivity analysis for projected, 37–38, 90
economy, 23; 1990s politics and, 11–20; agriculture of 1990s, 13–14, *15*, *16*, *17*; collapse of Tuareg, 12; revenue decline of 1997, 16, *16*
Egypt, Nile Basin Initiative and, 40
EIAS. *See* Environmental Impact Assessment Study
employment, 37
Environmental Impact Assessment Study (EIAS), 36, 38–41; complementary, 53–54; flooding risk and, 24; lack of data in, 18, 24; 2003 updated, 60
epidemiological studies, 39
Equatorial Guinea Cocoa Plantation Project, 26
ERR. *See* economic rate of return
ethnicity, 10, 27, 51
exports, 14, 16
external assistance, 2–3, 67–75, 95–96; conditions of, 73; foreign exchange portion of Program's, 32, *33*; Republic of Mali's current dependency on, 73. *See also* funding
externalization, conflict, 49–53, 67–75; negative impact of, 67–68, 71; upstream and downstream people response to, 95–96

face saving, 56, 64, 99
feasibility study, 4–5, 22, 23, 32; non-African company for, 24
field missions, Mali, 40
field supervision missions, 83–84
financial and economic analysis, 37–38
financial plan summary, *34*
first phase, 29–30, *33*, 36–37
flooding, 24, 33, 39
food security, 8, 28, 37
foreign exchange: portion of Program, 32, *33*; rates, 33, *33*, 89–90

foreign investment flow, 2–3
framing: conflict, 41, 52; Framework Law (Loi Cadre), 13, 47; modification in, 56; NGO perceptions and, 71–72; risk perception, 67
French colonial period, 9–10, 14, 28
funding: AfDF, 34, *34*, 35–36; disbursement, 84–89, *87*; international goodwill and, 27; OPEC, 33; organizations responsible for Program, 34, *34*; responsibility for approval of, 25. *See also* African Development Bank; external assistance

GDP. *See* gross domestic product
Ghana, gold mining project in, 69
Good Office Committee, 61–62, 81
government: decentralization, 12–14, 47; faith in, 22; show of concern by, 21–22. *See also* central government
gross domestic product (GDP), 14

Haut Conseil des Collectivites Territoriales (HCCT), 13
health issues, EIAS summary on, 39
high-context culture, 47–48, 49, 51, 53, 56, 72
Hirshleifer, Jack, 44, 46, 99
hydro-agricultural civil works: estimated cost summary for first phase, *33*; land development, 31; percentage of total cost dedicated to, 34
hydrological effects, 60

Idi Amin, 53
implementation, Program, 79–84; during conflict, 82–83; construction, 79–81, *80*, 82, 94; delay in, 38, 65, 94; of major activities, *80*, *81*
import totals, 14, 16
independence, 9
information and sensitization. *See* sensitization and information missions

international publicity, 94–95, 96–97, 98
International Water Management Institute (IWMI), 32
intervention, NGO, 18, 55, 59, 68–69; authority for, 70–71; invitations for, 69, 72; positive impact of C.S., 74. *See also* external assistance
irrigation: civil works, 31–32; Nile river abandoned project of, 40; potential, 11; source of Program area, 27
IWMI. *See* International Water Management Institute

Konare, Alpha Oumar, 12–13

land ownership, 45
lead time, 99
Loi Cadre (Framework Law), 13, 47
London 2012 Olympic Games Fund, 2
low-context cultures, C.S. as, 51, 71, 72

Mali: external assistance dependency of, 73; field missions to, 40; history and geography of, 9–11; location of, 2; major river basins of, *4*, 11, 23, 40, 41, 93; president of, 12, 64; size of, 10. *See also* Moyen Bani Program; *specific topics*
management, conflict, 53–56, 64
management team, 84, 100; AND and, 35
Manantali Dam, 33
Mato Oput (conflict resolution in tribal wisdom), 48
MCF. *See* Millennium Challenge Fund
MDD. *See* Mission de decentralisation et deconcentration
media, 47, 52–53, 63
mediator, 60, 61; Committee of Good Office meetings chaired by, 61–62; earlier involvement of, 98; functions of, 57; monitoring participation by, 88, 89; selection of, 56, 57; status of, 61

military coup, 12
Millennium Challenge Fund (MCF), 69
Mission de decentralisation et deconcentration (MDD), 13
missions: field, 40; field supervision, 83–84; sensitization and information, 54, 58, 62, 67, 81–82, 83–84
moderate complementarity, 45
modernization, 71
monitoring, Program, 82, 83–84, 88, 89
mosque, Djenne, 51
Moyen Bani Program (Program): additional studies in 2004, 63; approval date of, 45; area of, 3, 27–28, *29*; beneficiaries of, 28; cost and financial aspects, 31–34, 33, *34*; details, 28–31; economic and financial analysis, 37–38; financial plan summary for, *34*; increased scrutiny of, 88; major physical realizations of, *30*, 30–31; monitoring of, 82, 83–84, 88, 89; necessary interference in, 73–74; non-controversial activities of, 82–83, 87; objectives, 28–29; point of contention in, 1; political background of, 12–20; post-conflict period, 79; preparation and appraisal, 22–27; procurement and management, 35; rationale for, 21–22; technical preparation for, 3–4. *See also* conflict, Program; conflict resolution; costs; funding; implementation, Program; Talo dam
Mugabe, 53

neutrality, NGO, 70
NGOs. *See* nongovernmental organizations
Niger Basin Authority, 23
Niger River, 11, 27, 69; resource management of, 23; tributary rate of flow, 21
Nile Basin Initiative, 40
Nile River, 40

nongovernmental organizations (NGOs), 55, 68; conflict publicizing by, 52–53, 63, 69–70, 71, 74–75; Djenne-level dam and, 62; framing and perception issues, 71–72; neutrality of, 70; resource harnessing role of, 69. *See also* Association of Natives of Djenne; Cultural Survival; intervention, NGO

Office du Niger, 69
OPEC. *See* Organization of Petroleum Exporting Countries
Organization of Petroleum Exporting Countries (OPEC) fund, 33, 35–36, 52; disbursement from, 85, 86, *87*
overgrazing, 39

perceptions: Djenne people, 41; NGO framing and, 71–72; risk, 56, 65, 67; unique perception points, 44, 46; upstream population, 59. *See also* responses
political background, 12–20
politicization, 3, 5, 62, 66, 94–95
population: 1994 Program area, 27. *See also* downstream population; upstream population
post-conflict period, 79–92; implementation, 79–84, *80*, *81*, 94; monitoring during, 82, 83–84, 88, 89; sensitization and information missions, 81–82, 83–84
Poverty Reduction Strategy Papers (PRSP), 67
Poverty Support Program-2008, 86
preparation stage, 3–5, 22–27
procurement: AfDB suspension of, 50; management and, 35
production: cereals, 15, 16, *17*; delay, 38; goals, 28–29
Program. *See* conflict, Program; Moyen Bani Program
protest, early democracy and, 93
PRSP. *See* Poverty Reduction Strategy Papers

public image, AfDB, 55–56, 59
publicity: C.S. web site and, 52–53, 63; international, 94–95, 96–97, 98; NGO right of conflict, 69–70, 71, 74–75

rainfall, 10, 14, 21, 33, 93
rationale, Program, 21–22
reflective timing, 97
resources: conflicts over, 5, 43–46, 68–69; desire to acquire more, 99; NGO role in harnessing, 69; Niger River, 23
responses: externalization, 95–96; preparation stage identification of, 22–23, 25
revenue decline, of 1997, 16, *16*
risk perceptions, 56, 65, 67
river basins, in Mali, *4*, 11, 93. *See also specific rivers*
rural development projects: C.S. perceptions of, 71; external funding for, 2–3; international publicity on, 98; location issue for, 1–2; usefulness of studying, 6

screening processes, 7, 94. *See also* appraisal report
sedimentation, 40
Senegal River Basin, 41
sensitivity analysis: production delay not accounted for in, 38; for projected ERR, 37–38, 90
sensitization and information missions, 54, 58, 62, 67; post-conflict period, 81–82, 83–84
shareholders, AfDB, 25
Soyinka, Wole, 27
structural adjustment programmes, 18
studies: by Clark University, 68, 69; Comparative Irrigation Cost Study, 32; complementary, 53–54, 63, 65, 94; epidemiological, 39; feasibility, 4–5, 22, 23, 24, 32; rural development programs, 6; topographical data missing from, 18, 24. *See also* appraisal report; Environmental Impact Assessment Study
Sudan, 40
sunk cost, 47

Talo dam: completion of, 82; corner stone ceremonial for, 64; C.S. web site on, 52–53, 63; design modifications to, 81; flooding for adjacent regions, 33; negative framing of, 52; objectives for, 30, *30*, 33
Tanzania, 91
technical issues, 62–63, 68; technical preparation and, 3–4
third sector, development project, 70
Three Gorges Dam (China), 74
topographical data, EIAS lack of, 18, 24
Toure, Amadou Toumani, 12, 64
traditional cultures: conflict resolution in, 47–48, 49, 56, 68, 71; face saving in, 56, 64, 99
Traore, Moussa, 12
"triangulisation," 49–50, 51, 95–96
tribal wisdom, 48
Tuareg, 10, 12

UNESCO. *See* United Nations Education Scientific and cultural Organization
unique perception points, Hirshleifer's, 44, 46
United Nations Education Scientific and cultural Organization (UNESCO), 51
United States Agency of International Development (USAID), 53, 63, 68
United States of America (USA): conflict involvement of, 50; NGOs of, 55, 68, 69
upstream population: central government and, 58; ethnicity and culture of downstream and, 51; externalization response of, 95–96; flood impact

on, 39; AND mistrusted by, 58–59;
NGO intervention perceptions of, 59;
tension between downstream and, 56
USA embassy, 50
USAID. *See* United States Agency of
International Development

water flow, adequacy of: AfDB
reverting to issue of, 54; conflict
beginning with, 46, 49; conflict
breakthrough with, 62; Djenne
people concern of, 52
water quality, downstream, 39
Web Atlas on Regional Integration, 41
web site, C.S., 52–53, 63

yields, 21, 91. *See also* cereals

www.ingramcontent.com/pod-product-compliance
Lightning Source LLC
Chambersburg PA
CBHW030116010526
44116CB00005B/279